STAND & DELIVER:
THE LEE JEANS SIT-IN

Frances Poet

Stand and Deliver: The Lee Jeans Sit-In was first produced by National Theatre of Scotland and Tron Theatre Company. It premiered at the Tron Theatre, Glasgow on 28 April 2026.

STAND & DELIVER: THE LEE JEANS SIT-IN

Frances Poet

CAST

Aron Dochard	Finlay
Jo Freer	Helen
Madeline Grieve	Ensemble
Hannah Jarrett-Scott	Cathie
Shonagh Murray	Performing Musical Director
Chiara Sparkes	Maggie

All other parts are played by members of the company.

TEAM

Glenda Carson	Captioner
Christina Chappell	Technical Manager
Michelle Chambers	Wig/Hair & Make-up
Fee Dalgleish	Lighting Supervisor/ Programmer & Re-lighter
Paul English	Co-conceiver/Story Consultant
Craig Fleming	Production Manager
Bryan Gallagher	Deputy Stage Manager
James Gardner	Set Electrics
Suzanne Goldberg	Assistant Stage Manager (Rehearsals)
Chris Gorman	Sound Supervisor
Mickey Graham	Company Stage Manager
Emma Jones	Lighting Designer
Catherine King	BSL Interpreter
Jemima Levick	Director
Claire McKenzie	Arranger/Musical Supervisor
Christopher McKiddie	Audio Describer
Ruth Main	Wardrobe Supervisor
Ailsa Munro	Costume Supervisor
Jamie Murray	Lighting Supervisor
Kevin Murray	Sound Designer
Frances Poet	Writer
Jean Sangster	Voice Coach
Archie Scott	Swing Technician/Sound No 2
Yvonne Strain	BSL Interpreter
Eilidh Watt	Stage Management Placement
Chris Stuart Wilson	Choreographer
Jessica Worrall	Set and Costume Designer

CAST

Aron Dochard | Finlay
Aron plays DC Clark in the Netflix series *Department Q*. He trained at Rose Bruford College of Theatre and Performance.

Other television credits include: *Andor* (Disney+); *The Witcher: Blood Origin*, *Bodies* (Netflix).

Theatre credits include: *Tennessee Rose* (Pleasance Theatre); *Peter Pan* (Hull Truck Theatre); *Life Apparently* (Hoxton Hall).

Jo Freer | Helen
Jo has spent 25 years working in theatre in Scotland. She most recently appeared in the Tron Studio3 season in *Fleg and Fruitcake*. Some of her favourite work includes: *The Steamie, Sunshine on Leith, The Witches, Midsummer* and *The Cheviot the Stag and the Black, Black Oil* (Dundee Rep); *The Alchemist, Cinderfella* and *Alice in Weegieland* (Tron Theatre); *The House of Bernarda Alba, Mary Queen of Scots Got Her Head Chopped Off, Our Teacher's a Troll, Submarine Time Machine, Let The Right One In* (National Theatre of Scotland); *Bingo! The Musical* (Stellar Quines);*The Penny Drops, Made in China, The Company Will Overlook a Moment of Madness* (A Play, a Pie and a Pint),*Trumpets and Raspberries, Cinderella* (The Royal Lyceum); *Little Shop of Horrors, Absurd Person Singular, Communicating Doors, Amadeus* (Pitlochry Festival Theatre); *Seanmhair* (The Other Room); *SLICK* and *How to Steal a Diamond* (Vox Motus); *Trainspotting* (York Theatre Royal) and *Murmurations* (Tangled Feet).

Television work includes: *River City, Doctors, Scot Squad* (BBC) and *Emmerdale* (ITV).

Madeline Grieve | Ensemble
Madeline was born in Perth and trained at New College Lanarkshire.

Theatre credits include: *Starving, Ship Rats, Welcome to Bannockburn* (A Play, a Pie and a Pint); *Sinbad* (Perth Theatre); *Only In Our Dreams* and *Rapunzel* (Kapow Theatre); *Beauty and the Beast, Jack and the Beanstalk, Sleeping Beauty* (South Lanarkshire Leisure & Culture).

Film and television credits include: *Counsels* (Ballon Entertainment/BBC); *The Control Room* (Heartwood Films/BBC); *Nora Can't Score* (NFTS); *Time Teens* (Dreamcastle).

Hannah Jarrett-Scott | Cathie
Hannah trained at the Royal Central School of Speech and Drama.

Theatre includes: *The Little Mermaid*, *Peter Pan* (King's Theatre Glasgow); *Wild Rose, Glory on Earth, The Lion, the Witch and the Wardrobe* (Royal Lyceum Edinburgh); *Same Team* (Traverse Theatre); *Medea on the Mic, Alright Sunshine* (A Play, a Pie and a Pint); *Gunter* (Dirty Hare, Royal Court Theatre & Edinburgh Fringe Festival – winner of a Fringe First); *Burning Bright* (Òran Mór); *Underwood Lane, Cinderfella* (Tron Theatre); *Pride and Prejudice* *(sort of)* (Criterion Theatre, West End, UK Tour & Tron Theatre – winner of an Olivier Award); *The Taming of the Shrew* (Tron Theatre, Sherman Theatre); *The Wolves, Janis Joplin: Full Tilt* (Stratford East); *A Bottle of Wine and Patsy Cline* (Gilded Balloon); *A Stone's Throw* (Giddy Aunt); *Once This Is All Over We Still Have To Clear Up* (Yellow Magpies); *Midsummer Songs* (New Wolsey Theatre); *Lockerbie: Lost Voices* (Elements World Theatre).

Television credits include: *Outlander* (Sony/Starz/LeftBank); *Two Doors Down* (BBC Studios); *Float* – Series 1 & 2 (Black Camel Pictures for BBC); *Annika* (Black Camel Pictures for Alibi); *Scot Squad, Short Stuff* (BBC Scotland); *Trust Me* (Red Productions for BBC).

Radio and Audio credits include: *Hotline* (Tron Theatre); *Rebus, Playing the Odds* (BBC).

Hannah is a singer-songwriter; you can listen to her original music on Spotify.

Shonagh Murray | Performing Musical Director
Shonagh Murray is a musical director and composer/writer based in Glasgow; she trained at the Royal Conservatoire of Scotland.

As a musical director, Murray's credits include: *Ballad Lines* (Aria Entertainment & KT Producing, Southwark Playhouse, Elephant); *The Great Gatsby* (Pitlochry Festival Theatre & Derby Theatre); *Nessie* (Pitlochry Festival Theatre & Capital Theatres); *Oor Wullie* (Noisemaker, Dundee Rep Theatre); *Ceilidh* (Noisemaker, Foresight

Theatrical, Beth Williams, Barbra Whitman); *The Snow Queen* (Royal Lyceum Theatre); *Fantastically Great Women Who Changed The World* (Kick Ass Theatre Productions Ltd, Edinburgh Festival Fringe 2022 & deputy MD for UK Tour 2023); *God Catcher* (Prickly Pear Productions & Petrichor Productions, Edinburgh Festival Fringe 2023); *A Mother's Song* (Macrobert Art Centre & KT Producing); *Orphans* (National Theatre of Scotland, as Associate Musical Director).

Murray's most recent composer credits are *Nessie* (Pitlochry Festival Theatre & Capital Theatres); *Armour* (A Play, a Pie and a Pint); *Saturdays Doon The J.M* (Dundee Rep); *The Great Elf Escape: LIVE* (The Gaiety, Ayr); *Burns: A Lost Legacy* (Edinburgh Festival Fringe 2019, Fearless Players).

Chiara Sparkes | Maggie
Chiara trained at the Royal Conservatoire of Scotland and the Dance School of Scotland.

Her theatre credits include: *Rollers Forever* (Pavilion Theatre); *Mamma Mia!* (UK & International Tour); *Tally's Blood* (Scottish Tour), *The Glasgow Poisoner*, *Bridezilla and the Orchid of Sin* (A Play, a Pie and a Pint), *Glasgow Girls* (RAW Material UK & Ireland Tour 2019 and National Theatre of Scotland/Pachamama Productions UK Tour 2017); *So Long, Wee Moon* (Braw Clan); *The Snow Queen* (Noisemaker/Dundee Rep Theatre); *The Yellow on the Broom* (Dundee Rep Theatre); *Eddie & the Slumber Sisters* (Catherine Wheels Theatre Company/National Theatre of Scotland); *Mother Goose*, *Sleeping Beauty* (Ayr Gaiety Theatre), *Snow White* (PACE Theatre Company); *Thread* (Kick the Door); *Robin Hood* (Cumbernauld Theatre).

Screen credits include: *Scotland is Open* for the Scotland is Now Global Campaign (Forest of Black): *The Kids Are Alt Right* (Braw Clan): *The Famous Grouse* (Greenroom Films); *Logan High* (Chalkboard TV/BBC). She has also provided voice-over work for the Scottish Government and was awarded Young Scottish Musical Theatre Performer of the Year 2017.

TEAM

Paul English | Co-conceiver/Story Consultant
Inverclyde-raised journalist and broadcaster Paul English has covered arts and culture in Scotland and beyond for 28 years. His writing appears regularly in *The Times* and *Sunday Times*, *The Sunday Post*, *The Daily Record* and *The Herald* newspapers and *The Scots* and *Big Issue* magazines.. As a broadcaster his reports have featured on Radio 4's *PM*, *The World At One*, *The World Tonight* and Sunday programmes and a variety of BBC Radio Scotland programmes including *Sunday Mornings*, *Good Morning Scotland* and *Out of Doors*. Paul has presented STV travel series *Scottish Passport*, numerous BBC Scotland programmes including *Off the Ball*, *Afternoons*, *Mornings*, and a variety of live music shows, as well as documentaries including *Lost Letters* and *Travis: The Man Who at 20*. He is a regular contributing reporter and presenter on the station's daily arts and culture output. His official biography of Deacon Blue, *To Be Here Someday*, was released in 2021. He lives in Glasgow.

Emma Jones | Lighting Designer
Emma is a Lighting Designer based in Scotland.

Previous shows for the National Theatre of Scotland include: *Tero Buru*, *Lament for Sheku Bayoh* and *Enough of Him*.

Other credits include: *Arlington, Totentanz, Ferguson and Barton* (shotput); *The Great Gatsby* (Derby Theatre/Pitlochry Festival Theatre); *The 39 Steps* (Pitlochry Festival Theatre); *Auntie Empire* (Disaster Plan/Jordan and Skinner); *Not for Glory* (Charlotte Mclean and Jack Anderson); *Balfour Reparations* (Farah Salah); *These Mechanisms* (Christine Thyme and Robbie Synge); *Radiant Vermin* (Tron Theatre); *AUGUST* (National Dance Company Wales); *A History of Paper* (Dundee Rep/Traverse); *LUNA* (Birmingham Royal Ballet); *Sunset Song* (Dundee Rep/Royal Lyceum Theatre Edinburgh); *float* (Starcatchers); *Pirates!, The Life and Times, Dreamers, YAMA, MIANN, Velvet Petal, Ray, Antigone, Interrupted, Tutumucky* (Scottish Dance Theatre); *Futuristic Folktales, AND* (Charlotte Mclean and Collaborators); *And The Birds Did Sing* (Curious Seed); *Mother Goose, Aladdin, Jack and the Beanstalk, Cinderella* (Perth Theatre); *Through the Mud* (Stella Quines/Royal Lyceum Theatre Edinburgh); *Stornoway, Quebec* (Theatre Galore); *Fibres* (Stellar Quines/Glasgow Citz); *Lightning Ridge* (Catherine Wheels Theatre Company); *The Man in the Submarine* (Perth

Theatre/The Byre Theatre); *LENA* (Feather Productions); *The Emperor's New Clothes* (Derby Theatre/Hiccup Theatre/Polka Theatre); *Ode to Joy* (Stories Untold); *A Christmas Carol, Peter Pan, Cinderella, Hansel and Gretel, Alice in Wonderland* (Derby Theatre); *Midsummer, Talking Heads, The Little Mermaid* (Dundee Rep); *Equilux* (Danza Contemporanea de Cuba); *DÝRA* (SHHE); *Cinderella: A Fairy Tale* (Royal Lyceum Theatre Edinburgh).

Jemima Levick | Director
Jemima trained at Queen Margaret University College in Edinburgh and on a Scottish Arts Council Directors Bursary with the Royal Lyceum Theatre Edinburgh and Stellar Quines Theatre Company.

In April 2024 she took up post as Artistic Director of the Tron Theatre. She has also served as Artistic Director and Chief Executive of A Play, a Pie and a Pint, Artistic Director and Chief Executive of Stellar Quines Theatre Company, and Artistic Director of Dundee Rep.

She has won and been nominated for a number of awards and has directed over 50 professional productions. Her previous work with National Theatre of Scotland includes: *The 306: Day* (with Stellar Quines/Perth Theatre/Red Note Ensemble), *The Last Queen of Scotland* (with Stellar Quines) and *You Tell Me What Was, We Tell You What Is* (co-director). Other more recent directing credits include: *SCOTS* (a national tour for Raw Material, following an original production at A Play, a Pie and a Pint/Edinburgh Fringe/54 Below NYC); *Cinderella* (Royal Lyceum Theatre Edinburgh); *Man's Best Friend, A View from the Bridge, Fruitcake* (Tron Theatre); *The Sheriff of Kalamaki, Sally, Meet Me at The Knob, The Great Replacement, The Joke* (A Play, a Pie and a Pint); *Maggie May* (Leeds Playhouse/Leicester Curve/Queens Hornchurch); *All My Sons, Cinderella* (Dundee Rep) and episodes of *River City* for BBC Studios.

Claire McKenzie | Arrangements and Musical Supervisor
Claire McKenzie trained at the Royal Conservatoire of Scotland and is a Composer and Musical Director.

Her credits in theatre include: *SCOTS* (A Play, a Pie and a Pint/Edinburgh Fringe/54 Below, NYC); *Maggie May* (Leeds Playhouse); *Oor Wullie, A Christmas Carol, The Snow Queen, Little Red and the Wolf* (Dundee Rep); *The Lion, The Witch and the Wardrobe,*

The Caucasian Chalk Circle, *The Iliad*, *The BFG*, *Faith Healer*, *The Venetian Twins* (Royal Lyceum Edinburgh); *The Great Gatsby* (Off-Broadway); *My Left/Right Foot – The Musical* (National Theatre of Scotland); *Atlantic: A Scottish Story* (Winner of Best British Podcast Award for Drama); *Hi, My Name is Ben* (Goodspeed Musicals/ NAMT); *The Cook, The Thief, His Wife And Her Lover* (Faena Miami/Unigram); *A View from the Bridge* (Tron Theatre); *Legend Trippers* (National Youth Music Theatre); *Long Day's Journey Into Night*, *Hayfever*, *Hansel and Gretel*, *Beauty and the Beast*, *Cinderella* (Citizens Theatre).

Claire is also one half of the award-winning musical theatre writing team, Noisemaker. Future projects include *CEILIDH* (Barbara Whitman/Grove Entertainment – UK & US Tour); *The Snow Goose* (Goodspeed Musicals); *Hi, My Name is Ben* (LD Entertainment); *Porter* (Signature Theatre, DC /Fiasco Theater). Scott and Claire were recently awarded the 2025 Jonathan Larson Grant from The American Theatre Wing.

Kevin Murray | Sound Designer
Kevin Murray is a Sound Designer and composer with a Masters in Sound Design for the Moving Image, from the Glasgow School of Art. In 2016, he was awarded the BAFTA New Talent award for his original short film *Paperclip*.

Kevin has written music for numerous outdoor events, across the UK. He is currently Sound Designer and Composer for Itison's *Glasglow* in the Glasgow Botanic Gardens, now onto its seventh year.

Previous theatre work includes: Sound Designer for *The Outrun* by Stef Smith at the 2024 Edinburgh International Festival; Sound Designer for *Hamlet* with Ian McKellen at the Edinburgh Fringe 2022; Sound Associate for the National Theatre of Scotland; Sound Designer and composer for the Royal Conservatoire of Scotland's production of *A Christmas Carol*.

Frances Poet | Writer
Frances Poet is a Glasgow-based writer of stage, screen and radio.

Stage plays include: *Small Acts of Love* which reopened the newly renovated Citizens Theatre and was a finalist of the Susan

Smith Blackburn Award 2026, *Fruitcake* (Tron Theatre); *There Is No Room In Our Bathroom For Lewis Capaldi* (PACE at Paisley Arts Centre); *Sense and Sensibility* (Pitlochry Festival Theatre and OVO, St Albans); *Still* (Traverse); *Maggie May* (Leeds Playhouse/ Queens Theatre Hornchurch/Leicester Curve/Susan Smith Blackburn Finalist); *Fibres* (Citizens Theatre/Stellar Quines); *Gut* (Traverse Theatre/Tron Theatre, Writers' Guild Best Play) and the multi award-winning *Adam* (National Theatre of Scotland, Fringe First, The Flying Artichoke Award and, on screen, winner of BAFTA Scotland Best Television Scripted2020 and Audience Award for Best Film at the Vancouver Queer Film Festival).

Frances's work is often produced internationally with recent productions including a French translation of *Fruitcake* (Les Prémonitions De Mikaël Morneau, translated by Marc-André Thibault) produced in Montreal, two Turkish-language productions of *Gut* (His, translated by Servat Aybar) premiered in Istanbul and Cyrpus, a Portuguese translation of *Adam* produced in Lisbon (translated by Nuno Gonçalo Rodrigues) and *Crusaders* (NT Connections) produced at India's National Centre for Performing Arts.

Screen work includes a number of short films produced at national and international film festivals, two episodes of Black Camel's hit crime drama, *Annika* and several episodes of *River City*.

Frances has also written two five-part radio drama series with monolgues by Eileen Horne; *This Thing of Darkness* Series 4 and 3 (Finalist of the New York Festivals Best Drama Podcast). Both series are currontly available to listen to on BBC Sounds.

Jean Sangster | Voice Coach
Theatre includes: *Maggie and Me, Medea, The Enemy, The House of Bernarda Alba, The Bacchae* (NTS); *Make it Happen* (NTS, EIF & Dundee Rep); *Cyrano de Bergerac* (NTS, Royal Lyceum Theatre, Citizens Theatre); *The Steamie, The Bookies, Wings Around Dundee, Oor Wullie, The Yellow on the Broom, Deathtrap* (Dundee Rep); *Sunset Song* (Dundee Rep, Royal Lyceum Theatre); *Hindu Times* (Dundee Rep, Stellar Quines); *Moonset, Little Red Riding Hood, The Choir, Hay Fever* (Citizens Theatre); *Sunset Song, The Broons* (Selladoor Productions); *Backbeat* (Act Productions); *Heer Ranja, Fifty Shades of Black* (Ankur Productions).

Performance includes: *Size Matters* (Momoru Iriguchi prod. Vanishing Point); *Pirates!, Antigone, Interrupted* (Scottish Dance Theatre); *Lachez Tout!* (Red Note Ensemble & LOD muziektheater); *Hand Me Down* (Glass Performance) .

Jean is Head of Voice & the Centre for Voice in Performance CViP at the Royal Conservatoire of Scotland, an Artistic Associate in Voice at Dundee Rep and a keen advocate of Scots Language.

Jessica Worrall | Set & Costume Designer
Theatre Design work includes: *Black Diamonds & The Blue Brazil, The Girls of Slender Means* (Lyceum, Edinburgh); *Inexperience, Beautiful: The Carole King Musical, Group Portrait in a Summer Landscape* (Pitlochry Festival Theatre); *The Trials* (Tron Theatre); costume for *Small Acts of Love*; *Red Riding Hood, Comedy of Errors* (Citizens Theatre); *Doubt: A Parable* (Dundee Rep); *Henry IV parts 1 & 2, Henry V, Two Noble Kinsmen* (Shakespeare's Globe); *After Edward, Edward II, The Treason Trial of Walter Raleigh, The Captive Queen* (Sam Wanamaker Playhouse); *Educating Rita* (Dukes Theatre); *Rites* (National Theatre Scotland); *When We Are Married, She Stoops to Conquer, Love's Labour's Lost, School for Scandal* (Northern Broadsides); *The Last Straw, Ghost Sonata, The Obituary Show, A Song without Sound?* (People Show).

Film design includes: *The Last Day, The Jossers* (dir. Gareth Brierley/People Show) *Death of a Double Act* (dir. Christine Entwisle); *The Loss of Sexual Innocence* (dir. Mike Figgis).

Jessica also now works as a digital collage artist. You can follow her work on Instagram @jessicaworralldigitalcollage

Chris Stuart Wilson | Choreographer
Chris Stuart Wilson is a multi-disciplinary creative force whose work spans direction, choreography, performance, and socially engaged artistic practice. His choreographic career has seen him collaborate with leading companies across the UK, including the National Theatre of Scotland, Perth Theatre, Citizens Theatre, and Dundee Rep. From 2010–2018, he served as Resident Choreographer at Pitlochry Festival Theatre, shaping more than 30 major productions. His credits there include the award-winning *White Christmas, Singin' in the Rain,* and the record-breaking

Chicago. National tours include *Hen Night Horror*, *Rollers Forever*, and *To Save the Sea*.

A committed advocate for the transformative power of music and dance, he leads projects supporting vulnerable and marginalised communities. He was a facilitator on the National Theatre of Scotland co-production *Coming Back Out Ball*, celebrating the lives of LGBTQ+ elders, and this work continues through the Culture Club Collective. His dance work for people living with dementia has achieved international acclaim, featured in the BBC documentary *Dancing to Happiness* with Dame Darcey Bussell.

On the international stage, he is also celebrated for his acclaimed cabaret alter ego, *Jesus L'Oreal*, a genre-blending reinvention of the Messiah recast as a fitness and lifestyle influencer under the banner of "Jehovah's Fitness". @chrisjswilson

[NATIONAL THEATRE OF SCOTLAND] 20

We don't have our own venue. Instead, we're able to bring theatre to you wherever you are. From the biggest stages to the smallest community halls, we showcase Scottish culture at home and around the world. We have performed in airports and tower blocks, submarines and swimming pools, telling stories in ways you have never seen before. We want to bring the joy of theatre to everyone.

Since we were founded in 2006, we have produced hundreds of shows and toured all over the world. We strive to amplify the voices that need to be heard, tell the stories that need to be told and take work to wherever audiences are to be found.

To find out about the full team at National Theatre of Scotland please visit **nationaltheatrescotland.com/about/our-people** You can also follow us on:

Twitter	**@NTSOnline**
Facebook	**@NationalTheatreScotland**
YouTube	**@ntsonline**
Instagram	**@ntsonline**
TikTok	**@ntsonline**
Bluesky	**@ntsonline.bsky.social**

If you would like to give us feedback on the show, please email us at **feedback@nationaltheatrescotland.com**

SUPPORT US

Stand and deliver!

Or, stay seated and deliver.

Stick £20 in and join the merry band of supporters who make shows like this one possible.

To celebrate our 20th anniversary, every £20 donation also enters you into our monthly prize draw.

Join us: **nationaltheatrescotland.com/support**

National Theatre of Scotland is Core funded by the Scottish Government

TRON THEATRE

Established in 1982, Tron Theatre has built a national and international reputation for producing and presenting ambitious, contemporary and proudly subversive theatre, reflecting the world we live in and representing the people of Glasgow and of Scotland. We have established ourselves as a vital, creative hub for the Scottish theatre sector as a powerhouse of home-grown, contemporary Scottish work.

The Tron building, with its centuries-old heritage, stands proudly on the edge of the city, where the city centre meets the ever-changing east end of Glasgow. As well as the Tron's self-produced programme, it provides a critical cog in the UK's touring infrastructure, a vital incubator and supporter of emerging and mid-career talent, as well as facilitating vibrant participatory arts opportunities for people across the city.

Our artistic programme sees seasons of bold work that place us at the forefront of both creating and presenting high quality, ambitious theatre that represents and reflects the diversity of the world around us, both locally and globally. We aim to take people on a journey; entertaining, engaging, challenging and celebrating stories that encapsulate all perspectives of life.

The circular economy of our organisation's culture is paramount to our success, reaching into and investing in communities and working alongside participants, artists, schools, makers and audiences. Through learning from these stakeholders, we draw this back into the work we present, to build on the Tron's extraordinary history, expanding our touring offer and partnerships, as well as inviting a plethora of new and familiar artists and participants into the building. Now in its fifth decade, the Tron continues to innovate and grow, along with its audience.

To find out more about the Tron Theatre go to **tron.co.uk** or follow us on:

Facebook	**@trontheatre**
YouTube	**@trontheatre**
Instagram	**@trontheatre**
Bluesky	**@trontheatre.bsky.social**

If you would like to give us feedback on the show, please email us at **feedback@tron.co.uk**

SUPPORT TRON THEATRE

As a charitable organisation with a responsibility to our community, we are passionate about keeping ticket prices as low as possible. Therefore, we must raise additional funds in order to deliver a varied programme of high-quality, thought-provoking work that is affordable and accessible.

Donations enable us to run an extensive Participation programme for all ages, fund initiatives to support emerging talent, deliver outreach programmes in our local communities and give away hundreds of tickets to people experiencing disadvantage through our Pay It Forward initiative. Even the smallest donation will help secure the future of the Tron.

We are supported by Creative Scotland and Glasgow City Council.

If you would like to find out more about the different ways you can support the Tron Theatre, please visit **tron.co.uk/supporting_the_tron_theatre** or email **development@tron.co.uk**

Tron Theatre Lts id a Scottish Registered Charity No SC012081

STAND & DELIVER:
The Lee Jeans Sit-In

Frances Poet

Introduction
Dr Andy Clark

Stand & Deliver is a true story. I state that because it's
a remarkable story of grit, determination and solidarity in
a modern-day David vs Goliath battle. I've been incredibly
fortunate to have spent the last thirteen years researching the
Lee Jeans sit-in, speaking with those involved to understand
what happened, their motivations, their emotions, and to place it
within the broader story of Scotland's recent history. It's a story
I know inside out, and I'm excited that it's being brought to
a public audience in an engaging and entertaining production by
the National Theatre of Scotland and the Tron Theatre.

Lee Jeans was a subsidiary of the US-based VF Corporation.
The Greenock workers – mostly sewing machinists producing
Lee Jeans – were informed that their factory in the Larkfield
industrial estate would close in January 1981, a decade after
its doors had opened to much fanfare among Inverclyde's
politicians. The local authority had worked hard to attract VF
to the town. The firm received free rent and rates in their first
three years and a fifty per cent discount for the following three.
The government paid forty per cent towards the costs of plant
and machinery, and the Regional Employment Premium entitled
them to a payment of £2 per worker per week.

After a little over ten years in Greenock, VF sought to capitalise
on incentives elsewhere, namely Northern Ireland. It was not
unusual for multinational firms to seek to relocate production to
take advantage of the availability of new, and more generous,
subsidies. And, if we're to be fair to those at VF, it was
a sensible business judgement; enhanced state support would
lead to increased profits, which is ultimately the aim of any
private enterprise. The suffering and hardship of the workers
impacted did not factor into these decisions. It's a tale as old
as capitalism itself, and still takes place today. However, VF
did not countenance that the workers at the Larkfield estate

wouldn't stand for this, and would mount a militant campaign of resistance against the injustice of the decision. They could never have foreseen what happened next, the story you will learn about through this play.

For the workers, they were faced with two options. Accept the inevitability of closure, take their redundancy payments, and leave the factory in search of alternative employment. This was much easier said than done. Greenock – and Scotland – was suffering from the effects of recession and the longer-term deindustrialisation of the country's economic base. Throughout the first half of the 1980s, 613 manufacturing sites closed across Scotland, leading to the loss of 164,000 jobs. Unemployment in Greenock was fifteen per cent, much higher than the national average. For women, unemployment was fifty per cent higher than Scotland as a whole. But the other option – to occupy and fight back – would be very difficult and was extremely uncommon. Historians have shown that resisting closure was rare; the vast majority of workers accepted their fate and took redundancy, often advised to do so by their union representatives. At this time, large workplaces like Singer in Clydebank and Talbot in Linwood closed with minimal opposition by the organised and much more union-experienced workers. If they couldn't prevent the inevitability of capital movement, what chance did a group of women in Greenock have?

Yet, occupy and resist is what the workers at Lee Jeans did. They became a well-organised machine, maintaining the site, gathering support, and managing financial donations. The sit-in became a cause célèbre over the seven months that the workers were camped inside the plant. National figures like Michael Foot and Tony Benn came to offer their support. Local shipyard workers gave regular financial donations from their wages, and arrived en masse on the day of planned closure to prevent any attempt to remove the occupiers by force. The Lee Jeans workers travelled the length and breadth of Britain to visit workplaces and collect financial and moral support for their action. And – SPOILER ALERT – they were vindicated. In August 1981, the factory was saved and the remaining occupiers returned to their machines to produce denims for Inverwear Ltd.

If that was the end of the story of the Lee Jeans sit-in, it would
already be a remarkable event in modern Scottish history.
But it isn't. There's a very important postscript that further
enhances the significance of the workers' action. Because they
not only saved their own jobs, but they inspired other Scottish
women to do the same. In March 1982, workers at both Lovable
Bra in Cumbernauld and Plessey Capacitors in Bathgate –
overwhelmingly women – were informed that their workplaces
would close, adding them to the growing army of Scotland's
unemployed. Rather than accept these decisions and leave their
workplaces, they sought inspiration – and in the case of Plessey,
direct support and advice – from the Lee Jeans workers. And,
after their own sit-ins, these factories avoided closure as well,
with both sites being bought over and many jobs saved. As
a result, the number of jobs saved by the action of the workers
in Greenock wasn't the 140 who returned to their machines in
Larkfield. Adding those at Cumbernauld and Bathgate, a total
of 620 Scottish workers were saved from the dole queue at this
time of recession and depression.

This period of occupation should be regarded as one of the most
significant in the recent story of Scotland's working class. The
workers' actions should be as well known as the 1926 General
Strike or the 1984–85 Miners' Strike. The names of their
leaders – Helen Monaghan (Lee Jeans), Sadie Lang (Lovable)
and Ina Scott (Plessey) – should be as revered and celebrated
as Jimmy Reid, Keir Hardie, and John Maclean. This play is
another step towards that: to ensure that anyone with a passing
interest in Scottish history knows about the women activists
who fought for their communities and their class. And who,
unlike so many working-class heroes, won their battles, in the
most unlikely of circumstances.

*Dr Andy Clark is Lecturer in Scottish History at the University
of Stirling. He is the author of* Fighting Deindustrialisation:
Scottish Women's Factory Occupations, 1981–82.

Acknowledgements

This play only exists because of the 140 workers who stayed the course of a seven-month-long occupation to keep their jobs. The biggest thank-you is to all of them and especially the ones generous enough to meet with me and share their personal experiences: Catherine Robertson, Margaret Brown, Theresa Houston, and with special thanks to Helen Monaghan, Maggie Wallace and Cathie Wallace for also allowing me to represent them and their late loved ones in this play. Thanks too to Patrick Clark, who though only making a brief appearance in the play, represents the overwhelming support and solidarity the workers received from local men.

I am indebted to the many people who have fed into the development of this play: Paul English, Jemima Levick, Claire McKenzie, Caroline Newall, Rosie Kellagher, Jackie Wylie, Dominic Hill, Andy Clark, Andrew Rosthorn, Sophia Porter, Maureen Dalton, Neil Murray, Maureen Carr, Danielle Fiamanya, Neil John Gibson, Louise Haggerty, Yana Harris, John Macauley, Naomi Stirrat, Betty Valencia, Anita Vettesse, Dylan Wood, Leah Byrne, Ryan Hunter, Elidh Loan, Anna Russell-Martin, Louise McCarthy, Emma Mullen, Samuel Pashby, Isaac Savage, Andrew Still, Karen Young, Aron Dochard, Jo Freer, Madeline Grieve, Hannah Jarrett-Scott, Shonagh Murray and Chiara Sparkes.

Thank you too to the brilliant creatives and hugely supportive production teams of National Theatre of Scotland and the Tron Theatre.

Big love and gratitude to my gang, Richard, Peter and Elizabeth, who may not have shaped this play but have shaped me.

F.P.
April 2026

A Note on Music

This play was conceived to be a 'good night out' and from the beginning I was drawn to the idea of threading some banging hits from 1981 through the piece. This appealed for a number of reasons. Firstly, it felt like a great way to evoke the period. Irrepressible songs with a new-decade energy like 'Girls on Film', 'Kids in America' and 'Stand and Deliver' felt fitting for the young women workers of the factory who found their voice and a sense of agency through the occupation. But so too did those songs that hit hard because of the context in which they were played; the melancholic 'Working Class Hero', frequently aired on the radio in the months after John Lennon's assassination, and 'Ghost Town' by The Specials, written in response to the impact on communities of high unemployment and recorded at the time of the Brixton Riots.

Music was also hugely important to the workers at the time. The occupation lasted seven long months. Seven months of negotiations, public speaking (to the press and various visiting dignitaries), marching and raising funds. But with twelve-hour shifts, day and night, shared out between them, there were still a lot of empty hours. They filled their time with knitting, playing cards, and singing songs with lyrics written up on the walls. They devised new lyrics to Joe Dolce's chart-topping 'Shaddap You Face' with the plea: 'Don't shut up a the place'. They also used Phil Ochs's 1960s protest song, 'Links on the Chain', as a basis to chart the course of the occupation: 'Eight weeks ago we occupied the fuckin' factory flair. We barricaded the bosses in, and they're still fuckin' there.'

I'm glad we are able to present all these songs, although I do feel pangs of guilt about how very hard the company of actors are having to work over a short rehearsal period; coming together as a band while playing multiple characters is no mean feat. I hope, however, that anybody reading this script with an eye to producing it themselves will jump at the chance, without being inhibited or intimidated by the musical framing. Music rights can be obtained to present the play as we have (in which case the two ensemble members are crucial), but I believe the play can 'sing' without the singing.

The four central characters in this play are not invented characters. They are all real people who I was lucky enough to meet, with the exception of Finlay who died before I started the project but who came alive through Helen and Maggie's descriptions of him. The women I met are so authentically themselves, it wasn't hard to capture them on the page with all their humour, wisdom and courage. And theirs is a story that deserves to be told. It can be easy to feel despondent about the world, to feel we have no agency, no chance of fighting injustice or effecting change but what Helen, Maggie, Cathie, Finlay, Catherine Robertson, and the other workers in the Lee Jeans family, achieved against all odds is so hopeful. And the world will always need stories of hope, where the underdog wins, even if only for a short time. So with or without the songs, let's keep telling their story.

For Andrew from your Twister

Characters

HELEN MONAGHAN, *forty-four*
MAGGIE WALLACE, *nineteen*
CATHIE WALLACE, *twenty-one*
FINLAY MONAGHAN, *seventeen*
ENSEMBLE 1
ENSEMBLE 2

This text went to press before the end of rehearsals and so may differ slightly from the play as performed.

The Kids fae Greenock

HELEN *walks on stage. She is intimidated by the audience but dutifully makes her way towards a central mic to speak. The words don't come. She takes a step back from the mic. She looks around for support and, as if she has conjured her, MAGGIE strides on.* HELEN *is steadied by her presence and that of* FINLAY *and* CATHIE, *who* MAGGIE *signals to join them on stage.*

MAGGIE. Shall we sing them a song? What about that 'Kids in America' one – that's perfect for us.

HELEN. How's 'Kids in America' perfect for us?

MAGGIE. You're a kid at heart, eh, 'Elen. And anyway, it sets the scene.

HELEN. How? We're no fae America. We're fae Greenock.

FINLAY. She's got a point.

MAGGIE. Kim Wilde wisnae fae America either and it worked for her.

CATHIE. Should start with that Italian song. That was never off the radio when it was all kicking off.

FINLAY. Which one?

CATHIE. Shut your face.

HELEN. Finlay was just asking.

MAGGIE. Our Cathie means that godawful 'Shaddap You Face' song.

CATHIE. Joe Dolce – we should start with that.

MAGGIE. Aye, great plan, Cathie. Make their ears bleed before we've even started.

HELEN. Talking about starting…

MAGGIE. Cannae start without the others.

FINLAY. No sure all two hundred and forty of them will fit on this stage.

MAGGIE. They have to. Cannae tell it without them.

CATHIE. Mebbe we've got all we need?

FINLAY. Mammy's the only one that's really important.

CATHIE. And Finlay's the eye candy. All the women fancied him.

MAGGIE. You mean, you did.

CATHIE. I never. I just meant that mebbe that's why he's here. Why are you?

MAGGIE. I'm here for the laughs.

CATHIE. Aye, 'cause everything you did was stupid.

MAGGIE. Why are you here?

CATHIE. I… Well I…

HELEN. Your Cathie cooked and cleaned along with our Marie.

MAGGIE. We've got the wrong Cathie. We need Cath'rine Robertson. She got us all singing, wrote the lyrics on the walls, kept us all cheerful. She was the one you relied on to get donations and that, 'Elen. She was my partner in crime. We need her. No you.

CATHIE.…I organised rotas!

MAGGIE. You think they've come here for rotas? How many punchlines will that involve?

Knock knock. Who's there? Cathie with her rota.

How many rotas does it take to change a light bulb? I don't know, check the rota.

HELEN. Maggie! We need to…

She points to the audience.

MAGGIE. Fine. I'm no stopping you.

MAGGIE *pulls the mic over and plonks it down in front of the others.*

FINLAY. Don't look at me.

CATHIE. Me either. I wouldnae know what to say.

MAGGIE. Cath'rine would…

HELEN *reluctantly steps up to the mic.*

HELEN. It started with the Belgians.

MAGGIE. Starts with my stupid big sister coming to work at the factory.

Not helpful, Maggie…

HELEN. I got us into a union 'cause a the Belgians.

MAGGIE. Once your sibling's in the door, it's all arranged. You don't get a say in it. And you're supposed to be grateful 'cause a bunch a your mates with nae big sister cannae get nae work at all.

HELEN. They were letting girls go who hadn't did their training. You cannae sack a girl for no doing her numbers when she's no been learnt the job properly.

MAGGIE. I wisnae grateful. I cannae sew. I was always put outside in sewing class.

HELEN. This is long before the Americans took over. I got us in a union and became shop steward. I didnae want to but they Belgians gied me no choice. Believe it or no, I didnae like making trouble.

MAGGIE. I made trouble in class 'cause I hated it. Leave school and find mysel sewing as a job.

HELEN. I liked my job. I liked things quiet.

MAGGIE. I was like a fish on a bicycle. I wisnae able to do my numbers, never mind doing enough to get my bonus. Folk after me in the line were complaining 'cause I'd got this or that wrong and I was slowing them down. I was on my final warning, this close to getting my books and becoming the newest member a Greenock's biggest growing club: The Unemployed. But 'Elen, she sat down with me.

HELEN. My job is to examine the work and get it boxed so I'm the one who has to go back to a worker if the quality's off. That's how I knew a lot a the girls and became somebody they trusted to tell them what's what.

MAGGIE. She telt me.

HELEN. You can do this.

MAGGIE. I don't want to do this. I don't even want to be in this factory.

HELEN. All they folk out there looking for a job and you're wanting to throw this one away?

MAGGIE. I'm nae good at it.

HELEN. I fought for girls like you to get their training. So stop panicking and listen to what your trainer is telling you. I *know* you can do this, Maggie.

MAGGIE (*to us*). And I did.

See, in a factory like this, / you're part of a team. You're a family.

HELEN. When / you're part of a team, you're a family – you have to speak up when things aren't right. You have to put up a fight.

MAGGIE. That's how it felt so wrong when they wanted to take it away. No 'cause I loved sewing. But 'cause these women were my family.

HELEN. The Americans were different altogether fae the Belgians. Smooth, wanting to offer us gold stars for good performance – I said to them, 'The only gold we want is what you can put in our hands.' By January 1981 we'd had ten years a the Americans. We'd had no trouble in that time. The trouble was all ahead a us.

The Factory

MAGGIE *leads the ensemble in pulling together a makeshift factory.* MAGGIE *hands out bits of trouser fabric.*

MAGGIE. Parts.

HELEN. Parts? Oh…

Parts.

The ensemble build a sense of the factory soundscape by naming the various parts getting made up.

FINLAY. *Two front legs.*

CATHIE. *Two front pockets.*

WORKER. *Two back legs.*

WORKER 2. *Two back pockets.*

FINLAY AND CATHIE. *Wiggly line and zips.*

HELEN. *Bundle boy. Moving the dolly.*

All of them follow the imagined bundle boy walking right to left along the line.

FINLAY. *Checking the machines. Oil them. Hone them. Polish them.*

CATHIE. *Press.*

HELEN. *Side seaming.*

WORKER. *End seaming.*

WORKER 2. *Stitch in the tab.*

FINLAY. *Press.*

CATHIE. *Waist… Waist… WAIST…!*

MAGGIE, *having established the line-up and removed herself, now comes running in and throws herself into work with impressive speed.*

MAGGIE. I'm here, I'm here! (*To* CATHIE.) You could a woke us up.

CATHIE. I shouted for you until my throat was sore. Not my fault you were late.

MAGGIE. I wouldnae have been late if you'd held the bus. Had to hitch a lift with that grumpy one who works at the semiconductor plant next door.

CATHIE. *Waist…*

MAGGIE *moves quickly to get into position.*

MAGGIE. *Bands.*

CATHIE *and* MAGGIE. *Chop.*

HELEN. *Bundle boy. Moving the dolly.*

All of them watch the imagined bundle boy.

HELEN. *Band ends.*

CATHIE. *Belt loops.*

MAGGIE. *Buttonholes.*

FINLAY. *Buttons.*

WORKER. *Ribbons.*

WORKER 2. *In-seaming.*

HELEN. *Cuffs and quality. Plastic wrap. Into the box.*

They all look out to the audience and with their best American accents recite the TV ad motto of the time…

ALL. *Lee. GenUine jeans. We brand every pair.*

And they're back to working.

HELEN. How is it, Maggie Wallace, that your sister can get herself to Larkfield on time and you cannae?

FINLAY. It cannae be that you spend more time getting ready.

MAGGIE. Are you saying I don't make the same effort as my sister?

FINLAY (*embarrassed now*). It's just – She – Well, she –

MAGGIE. 'Cause you'd be right, Finbar. They Farrah Fawcett-Major curls take our Cathie hours.

CATHIE. You shut up about my curls. My man loves them.

MAGGIE. Whereas I've got it so as I can get out the house in five minutes after waking. I lay out all my clothes, shoes all polished, overalls ready. Quick wash and a brush and I'm out.

CATHIE. Your hair hasn't seen a brush since our mammy put you in pigtails.

FINLAY. If it only takes you five minutes to get ready why are you the one that's always late?

MAGGIE. Well what it is, you see, Finlay, is that our dad sets our alarm for six but… there's seven of us. Ba-dum ching!

Tumbleweed.

(*Breaking out of the scene.*) That's not right. You've to act it out the way it happened. Folk laughed at that.

FINLAY. Mebbe the first time…

CATHIE. Aye, stopped being funny when you said it every single day.

MAGGIE (*back in the scene but determined to get her revenge*). Were you out singing last night?

CATHIE. Me?

MAGGIE. Aye, Cath'rine Robertson, you.

CATHIE (*breaking out of the scene*). Do I have to pretend to be folk I'm no?

HELEN. Don't ask me.

MAGGIE. How else are we gonnae show them what it was like? We've to build a sense a the whole factory.

…Were you out singing with your band, Vegas?

CATHIE *does not want to become Catherine Robertson.*

CATHIE. Cath'rine just stepped out but aye she said she was singing with Vegas last night.

MAGGIE. Where?

CATHIE. At the Upper Port Glasgow Social Club. Apparently hardly anybody showed. Folk are feeling the pinch – no going out midweek but she's hoping there'll be a good crowd at the Unity Club come Saturday. You should ask if you can be one a her backing singers, Maggie.

MAGGIE. Do you reckon?

CATHIE. It's closest you'll come to being in Vegas.

MAGGIE. Who said I want to go to Vegas? All they casinos are no for me. I like my chips Greenock-style – out the paper.

FINLAY. Her on side-seaming just finished telling me she's away to see Elvis singing there.

HELEN. Does she no know that Elvis 'left the building' four year ago?

CATHIE. She'll have to see Neil Diamond instead.

FINLAY. I didnae have the heart to tell her for fear she didnae end up looking like an Elvis song.

MAGGIE AND CATHIE. 'All Shook Up'!

FINLAY. I was thinking 'Heartbreak Hotel' but yours is better!

HELEN. Greta's on the prowl. Mebbe we should have a bit less blue suede and a bit more blue denim…

They work.

MAGGIE. Gonnae put the radio on, Finlay.

CATHIE. Please, no.

MAGGIE. How no? Bit a music to work to.

CATHIE. It's back-to-back John Lennon songs.

MAGGIE. You love John Lennon.

CATHIE. Aye, that's the problem. It's a constant reminder that some crazy idiot shot him. I can only listen to his songs now if I want to be sad.

FINLAY. First Ian Curtis, then Lennon. 1980 did not live up

to the 'new decade' hype folk were giving it. Never been so glad to see the back of a year.

MAGGIE. 1981'll be better.

HELEN (*breaking out of the scene*). Who's gonnae play Wee Bob Charters then?

CATHIE. Don't let Maggie loose on that accent.

FINLAY. I could gi' it a go?

MAGGIE. We're no doing Charters yet.

HELEN. But all a this is about Charters, Maggie. The day he came in.

CATHIE. Aye, us, optimistic, looking forward to a better year when he comes in to ruin it.

MAGGIE. You're skipping ahead. First you were slowing down deliberate so you wouldnae pick up the corduroy bundle.

CATHIE. I never.

MAGGIE. You did it that day and every day. Get nae bonus when you get stuck wi' the corduroy so you would kid on there was something wrong with your machine so I'd get cord and you could work quick with the denim. One minute it'd be your spools that were slipping, next minute, your machine was losing pressure.

CATHIE. My machine *was* always losing pressure!

MAGGIE. How come mine never?

CATHIE. My machine didnae work as good as yours. And we all know why that was.

ALL. Jimmy Denny.

HELEN. The head mechanic.

FINLAY. He was learning me the job.

MAGGIE. Twice my age. Divorced. I liked Jimmy.

CATHIE. And the rest.

MAGGIE. No. There was nothing between us. My mammy wouldnae allow it, no to mention our brother.

CATHIE. They weren't in the factory, were they? Naebody to stop you flirting.

MAGGIE. Flirting. He'd only have to look in my direction and youse would all start singing 'Young Girl' by Gary Puckett & The Union Gap.

FINLAY *and* CATHIE *start to sing it…*

MAGGIE *stops them with a look.*

CATHIE. He had your machine gleaming like a Rolls-Royce he'd find that many excuses to work on it.

FINLAY *becomes* JIMMY.

JIMMY. Alright Maggie. You wanting me to check your spools, aye?

MAGGIE. My spools are perfect, Jimmy. It's hers. Finlay checked them and cannae see what the problem is.

JIMMY. That's 'cause he keeps forgetting what I've telt him, don't you, Finlay lad – you've to look at the big picture when it comes to these machines.

MAGGIE. What did he miss?

JIMMY. That bundle a corduroy sitting there, for starters. It's a strange phenomenon. Machines work like Ferraris till there's cord lined up as the next bundle.

HELEN. I think you can make yoursel useful somewhere else now, Jimmy.

JIMMY. See you, Maggie.

MAGGIE. See you, Jimmy.

JIMMY *'exits', becoming* FINLAY.

HELEN. When are you two gonna stop feuding over cord?

MAGGIE. When are you gonnae ask management how we keep getting more cord than denim?

CATHIE. Aye, isn't that what the shop steward's supposed to do?

HELEN. If you two are no happy with me as shop steward, why don't you put yourselves forward?

MAGGIE. I didn't mean /

CATHIE. I wouldnae /

HELEN. No. Every time I try to sort out a second steward to represent you all, I get zero volunteers. You lot seem happy enough with how I'm representing you then.

MAGGIE. We're happy, 'Elen. Very happy.

CATHIE. Aye. And anyway, I asked Alec Anderson about the cord and he said naebody knows why.

HELEN. Why are you asking our machine-maintenance man about fabric?

CATHIE. 'Cause Alec's married to a supervisor! I thought Greta would a told him.

HELEN. Greta wouldnae know. Supervisor or no, she just does what Wee Bob Charters tells her.

FINLAY. Then why don't we ask him?

HELEN. I already have. Got nae answer. Charters just does what VF Corporation tells him to anyway so if we really want to know why, we'll have to write a letter to America. But feel free to ask him when he's next over fae Northern Ireland.

FINLAY. He's here the noo. Telt us to get word round all the sections that we're wanted for a meeting.

What's wrong, Mammy? Look like you just saw Basil Fawlty goose-stepping across the factory flair.

HELEN. Charters is no due here this month.

FINLAY. Aye well I wisnae gonnae tell him he wisnae welcome. He's the manager.

HELEN. What's he wanting all two hundred and forty of us thegither for?

MAGGIE. You say it like he's planning to line us up and shoot us?

CATHIE. Aye, how do you know he's no gonnae just wish us all Happy New Year?

HELEN (*to the audience*). Happy New Nothing. There's all
these questions nagging at me. Moving the cutting room to
Northern Ireland so the denim has to be shipped back here
to get made up. I said to them at the time: 'You're always
talking about how much it costs to make a pair a jeans.
Well it'll cost double now.' And then they sent my Marie
and some other lassies out to train up some a the Northern
Ireland lot. They make sweaters, see. They don't know
about jeans. They telt me to my face that was nothing to
worry about. And it's busy here – there's this huge order
that they're pushing us to get sent out quick. So I figure they
must know what they're doing, getting big orders, expanding
their operation. But if that's the case how are they getting us
working with worse and worse fabric and how do they keep
stalling about our yearly raise?

I'm no a gambling woman but my bet is that whatever
Charters is here to tell us has nothing to do with a happy new
year.

Fashion

Up steps BOB CHARTERS (*played by whoever in the
ensemble has the best Northern Irish accent*). *This isn't
a naturalistic moment.* BOB CHARTERS' *voice might be
sonically distorted and the response from the assembled might
be choreographed in some way. In the original production,
this speech was intercut with a performance of David Bowie's
'Fashion'.*

BOB CHARTERS. We have an over-capacity issue with the
factory here at Larkfield estate. This is as a result of the high
value of the pound. Sales from key buyers in Scandinavia
and other European countries are in decline. The factory is
no longer viable. We have no choice but to close the factory
and give all two hundred and forty of you notice of your
ninety days' redundancy. April 30th will be everybody's

last day in this factory. Though there will, of course, be a period of consultation first. Take the week to explore options. Happy New Year.

Economics

HELEN *chases after* BOB CHARTERS.

HELEN. This makes nae sense to me.

BOB CHARTERS. It's economics. It's not always easy for people to get their heads around.

HELEN. I'm nae good on economics, Bob. Explain it again slowly.

BOB CHARTERS. This factory just isn't profitable any more, Helen.

HELEN. And that's no because you moved the cutting room to Northern Ireland?

BOB CHARTERS. No, not at all. We were still turning a profit after moving that. This is bigger than us. It's about North Sea oil, the high value of the pound impacting global sales and the new government's free market policy /

HELEN. Ah, right, yes. So it's all Maggie Thatcher's fault?

BOB CHARTERS. It's complicated. It takes time to steady the ship as you turn it.

HELEN. Thought Maggie Thatcher said she wisnae 'for turning'?

BOB CHARTERS. She's not for turning on the issue of turning the ship. She's defeating inflation even if it means industry suffers in the short term. It's the economy she's turning around.

HELEN. Aye, industry suffers. And that's how you're closing us down – all because a the high value of the pound?

BOB CHARTERS. Exactly.

HELEN. And tell me, because you live there and I don't. What currency do Northern Ireland use?

BOB CHARTERS. The pound. But /

HELEN. And these charts that you have plastered all over this office that show how our factory is more profitable than the one in Northern Ireland, what do they mean?

The ensemble hold up charts right in BOB CHARTERS *face – he struggles to avoid them.*

BOB CHARTERS. They're out of date. We need to stop looking backwards, Helen.

He grabs them and scrunches them up.

HELEN. You're probably right. 'Cause if I was to look backwards, I'd think about all the money our government's dolled out to the Americans. Money that paid for the machinery sitting in there and gied them this place rent-free for ten year. Taxpayers' money. And they incentives have run out now. Now it's Northern Ireland that are offering rent-free.

BOB CHARTERS. This isn't about rent /

HELEN. Course not. The Americans wouldnae throw away hundreds a jobs they were gied money to create here in Scotland so that they can take handouts somewhere else? All so they get richer while we're left with nothing. That would be corrupt. Our provost who's head a the council who gied they grants would have something to say about that, would he no?

BOB CHARTERS. I'm telling you, Helen, this isn't about subsidies.

HELEN. No. It's about the high value of the pound.

BOB CHARTERS. That's right.

HELEN. You said we could present options. A period of consultation, you said.

We'll work a reduced week. Three days. And since we are already more profitable than Northern Ireland, and they Americans wouldnae dream of subsidy-hopping, there's nae reason whatsoever to go to the expense of moving all our equipment over there.

BOB CHARTERS. A three-day week?

HELEN. Or job-shares. Whatever gets us through.

BOB CHARTERS. I don't think /

HELEN. There must be a number, Bob. A maximum sum that you can afford to pay in wages and still turn a profit even with less orders. You're the economics expert, you tell us the number and we'll work to it with shorter weeks and job-shares. And then, when Maggie turns the ship, we can all two hundred and forty of us get back to work as normal. We're no wanting a single redundancy letter. Speak to your bosses. We're ready to sit down and make a deal soon as they are.

The scene shifts.

WORKER. A three-day week and job-shares? Some folk here are the main breadwinners, that'll put them in the red.

WORKER 2. And the rest a us. Food's expensive enough as it is.

FINLAY. She's calling their bluff.

HELEN. Aye and no. Once the jobs go, that's it. Drummonds is laying people off. Paton and Baldwins laid off even more before that and what about they that were let go of fae the Sugar House last summer? Naebody fought for they jobs and now there's hundreds a unemployed out hunting for work. Reckon they'd jump at even three days, don't you? This is Greenock. Sugar and ships and no enough jobs in either industry left for any a us. We need to hold on to these jobs even if it means sacrifices in the short term.

FINLAY. They've been working a three-day week at Linwood car plant since last summer. Seems to be working for them.

CATHIE. Well bully for Linwood.

MAGGIE. Will they say yes?

CATHIE. The *Greenock Tele* disnae think so. 'New Jobs Blow for District: Larkfield firm to close with two hundred and forty redundancies.'

CATHIE *proffers the* Greenock Telegraph.

HELEN. The journos there don't know what we're offering.

MAGGIE. Aye, how can they say no with an offer like that on the table?

HELEN. They'd have to admit that this isnae about profitability, it's about getting as many handouts as possible so they can squeeze out the maximum profit for their shareholders.

CATHIE. It's highway robbery is what it is.

HELEN. How can they admit to that?

FINLAY. But what if they don't care about that. What if they say no anyway? How are we gonnae stop them shifting all our machinery to Northern Ireland and our jobs with it?

HELEN. They're no gonnae say no.

They all look to the audience…

ALL. They said no.

HELEN. We got all two hundred and forty workers thegither in the canteen before the final consultation meeting. I telt them the plan me and the committee had come up with – 'If management say no to all our offers, we make a barricade between us and them in their offices' – but I never thought, I never believed…

They were all waiting on me walking out a that office wi' good news.

MAGGIE. Well?

CATHIE. What did they say, 'Elen? Did they agree?

FINLAY. Mammy?

HELEN *shakes her head.*

CATHIE. The *Greenock Tele* had it right then. All two hundred and forty jobs gone for good. There'll be nae work left for Greenock folk.

FINLAY. 'Cept for the posties – they'll have their work cut out delivering hundreds of redundancy letters.

MAGGIE. No, we're fighting it. Aren't we, Helen? Barricade the doors, that's what you said. The only way management can get to the machinery, the fabric, the orders needing doing is through they doors. They cannae gi' away our jobs without what's in there. That's what you said.

HELEN. Aye.

MAGGIE. So let's get stacking these chairs. Stop them getting through.

FINLAY. Mammy?

HELEN. I don't know, I… Just let me think.

MAGGIE. What's to think about?

HELEN. There's a lot to think about, Maggie Wallace. This isnae a game. This is two hundred and forty people relying on me. To do this right, to make the right decisions.

MAGGIE. Aye, to keep our jobs. We cannae let them take all this away, 'Elen.

In the original production, MAGGIE *sang the intro of 'Kings of the Wild Frontier' by Adam and the Ants here and made use of the family lyric. Here she might simply speak into the mic.*

We're a family.

MAGGIE *pinches* CATHIE *into speaking into the mic.*

CATHIE. We're a family.

She holds the mic to FINLAY *who obliges…*

FINLAY. We're a family.

MAGGIE *holds the mic to* HELEN. *She doesn't speak.*

MAGGIE. 'Elen?

FINLAY. It's up to you, Mammy.

CATHIE. Whatever you think is right.

HELEN. Aye, we're a family. We'd better get to it then.

Queens of the Wild Frontier

They move the furniture to a strong percussive beat, piling the chairs high. It's choreographed and full of attitude, with an unruly, feral quality. It may be that the percussive element remains through the next speeches, giving a sense of nervous anticipation.

HELEN. What comes next is / chaos.

MAGGIE. / Chaos and I love it.

HELEN. I've forgotten the word. What they call it when you strike without your union leadership sanctioning it. I'm on the payphone, trying to get through to our rep – I need to know our union have our back but he's no answering.

MAGGIE. Place is fizzy wi' nerves and excitement. I've no been this hyped up since J.R. got shot on *Dallas*. The queue for the payphone stretches as long as a traffic jam on a Friday night. Each a them taking their turn to put in their two-pence piece and tell folk what's going on. Their faces as pale as flour in a bakery.

WORRIED QUEUER (*dropping two pence in a metal bin*). I know I'm late, love. Can you put your daddy on for me?

WORRIED QUEUER 2 (*two pence*). Don't start bawling at me until I tell you what's happening.

WORRIED QUEUER 3 (*two pence*). Mammy, I'm no coming home the night. You'll need to keep the weans at yours.

ANGRY QUEUER. 'Elen said folk wi' dependents first. Your kids've no been dependent on you for years. Out the queue now.

ANGRY QUEUER 2. I have dependents /

ANGRY QUEUER. Cats don't count.

HELEN. Wildcat. That's the word. A labour strike initiated by workers without the authorisation or approval of their union leadership.

MAGGIE. I feel bad really 'cause I can see they're all worried but I just feel pure excited to be at the centre of it all. Excited… and hungry. The kitchen was all closed up for the day before 'Elen came out shaking her head. And since we've barricaded out the only folk who have a key, it's nae kitchen for us, no even a cup a tea. Cath'rine Robertson makes hersel' popular by handing out a pack a Rolos until she admits she found them in a box a threads at the back a the factory. Everybody's spitting them out. Cath'rine's hilarious. My belly's pure empty.

HELEN. My belly's full of snakes. Our union have been cautious since Thatcher's new legislation eighteen month ago. Called the Employment Act but it's really just her taking an axe to rights we were gied by the Labour government.

Polis have turned up and I can see Charters outside the factory talking to them, waving his arms about. I march Patricia Arkley up to the front a the phone queue.

MAGGIE. My mouth's watering for Aldo's chips and vinegar.

HELEN. Tricia's dad's big in trade unions.

MAGGIE. There's nothing like knowing you cannae eat to make you feel a raging hunger.

HELEN. I need some support here.

MAGGIE. Tangy and greasy and crisp and salty and soggy all at once.

HELEN (*to* MAGGIE). Will you gi' over?!

MAGGIE. What?! I'm hungry.

CATHIE. Me too.

FINLAY. Aye. I only had a small piece for my lunch and that was seven hour ago.

HELEN (*to us*). I'm hungry an' all and I'm thinking mebbe the next call should be to somebody who can get us some proper supplies.

That's when the phone jams.

MAGGIE. All they two-pence pieces. Normally disnae get this much action in a month, our payphone.

FINLAY. And only management have the key to empty it.

HELEN. It's no in their interest to empty it the now.

CATHIE. That's that then. We all go hungry.

MAGGIE. Nah, I'll pop to Aldo's.

HELEN. How you gonnae do that when the polis are standing outside?

CATHIE. The polis?! Are they coming in? Dragging us out?

HELEN. Disnae look that way.

CATHIE. They'll be Greenock lads.

HELEN. Greenock lads or no, they're hardly gonnae let Maggie swan out the door to get us all some chips.

MAGGIE. I'll no be swanning out the door, will I? I know a special way. There's a wee door in the garden I've watched they plumbers use when we get blockages in the toilets. I can get out, up the drain pipe, over the roof and into the car park.

CATHIE. She's pure sneaky, 'Elen. It's her one talent. I reckon she'll manage it.

FINLAY. And we'll need something in our bellies if we're staying here all night…

MAGGIE. I'll get a kitty thegither for chips for all a us. Margaret Brown already said she'd spot us wi' the cash she has on her to buy her mammy's messages. I can get to Aldo's, I know I can.

HELEN. Aye, but can you get back? Sneaking passed the polis wi' enough chips for an army?

MAGGIE. Where there's a will there's a way.

HELEN. Aye, alright.

FINLAY. Don't get caught.

CATHIE. Or fall to your death.

HELEN. Straight there and back, Maggie. You hear me?

Maggie's Mammy

One of the company becomes MAGGIE'S MAMMY.

MAGGIE'S MAMMY. Bloody hell've you been? Your tea's ready. Where's the other yin?

MAGGIE. She's still in the factory, Mammy. Look, I'm just here while Aldo bags up our chips. We're doing a sit-in.

MAGGIE'S MAMMY. Is that overtime, aye?

MAGGIE. No! A sit-in.

MAGGIE'S MAMMY. I'll sit-in you. Your tea's in that oven and it's ruined. How many times have I tellt you to come straight home on a Thursday and put your keep money on the top a that fridge-freezer.

MAGGIE. We didnae get our wages. That's what I'm trying to tell you. They're laying us all off but we're no gonnae let them. We're making a stand, occupying the factory. But the phone's jammed so we've no contact with anybody. Get on to STV will you and tell them what's happenin'.

MAGGIE'S MAMMY. And say what? 'Hello STV, it's me, Margaret Wallace's mammy – you're needing to get a film crew to Larkfield estate pronto.'

MAGGIE. Disnae matter whose mammy you are so long as

they know what's going on. And anyway, what's wrang wi'
being Margaret Wallace's mammy? Margaret Wallace's
mammy gets things done. Always has. She's the reason
Margaret Wallace didnae think twice about climbing over
a wall the night to get folk their tea. Margaret Wallace's
mammy's pure brilliant.

MAGGIE'S MAMMY. Aye alright then.

MAGGIE. See you when we've won this thing.

MAGGIE'S MAMMY. How long will that be? Maggie?
    Maggie!

Show Them We're Fighting

HELEN. Where the hell is she?

CATHIE. She's messed it up. She messes everything up.

FINLAY. She's there.

CATHIE. Oh hell, the polis have stopped her. Are they gonnae
    arrest her?

HELEN. I shouldn't have let her go.

CATHIE. She's talking a lot. Pointing a lot. She's opening one a
    the bags a chips and handing them round.

FINLAY. They're waving her through.

HELEN. You're kidding?

FINLAY. She's charmed them.

CATHIE. Get away wi' murder that yin. Always has.

FINLAY. You reckon the polis'll gi' her a leg-up while they're
    at it?

    MAGGIE *'s back.*

MAGGIE. Get your lippy on, 'Elen – STV are on their way!

HELEN. You what?

MAGGIE. Aye. How great is that?

HELEN. I'm no speaking to them.

MAGGIE. How no? What's the point of us making a big stand if naebody knows about it? All folk out there know is what the *Greenock Tele* tells them – that the jobs are gone and we've lost. Don't we need to show them we're fighting it?

HELEN. Maggie, this'll all be decided one way or another in less than twenty-four hours.

MAGGIE. How?

HELEN. Management will either sit down wi' us or they'll have us removed.

MAGGIE. Well they might think twice about having us removed wi' the cameras rolling out there. You should get over there and tell the world how stupid the managers are being.

HELEN. I'm wanting to sit down wi' management and make them see they should accept our offer. How'm I gonnae do that if I've been bad-mouthing them on the national news? Who got STV here anyway?

Gulp.

You just went to Aldo's and straight back? You didnae stop off anywhere in-between? Maggie?

She did.

Maggie! Think before you act, will you.

MAGGIE. I am thinking. I got them here and I'm no sorry. I'm gonnae to speak to them even if you willnae.

HELEN. It wisnae sorted in twenty-four hours.

We slept that night in our work clothes on bits a cardboard on a cold flair telling ourselves we could manage one night. Then we did it again and again. Management didnae sit down wi' us but they didnae throw us out.

MAGGIE. Aye, 'cause a they cameras.

HELEN. Mebbe. But cameras or no, after three long nights locked in we were all pretty much at the end of our tether.

Doors and Bars and Metal

In the original production, the ensemble launched into the brilliantly preposterous Bay City Rollers' vocal opening to 'Doors, Bars, Metal'. Whatever is chosen here should be stylised and can afford to be absurd/comedic. They hold up various bits of cardboard and bedding. They read: 'THREE DAYS IN'.

A soundscape of complaints and moaning layers up. HELEN *is feeling harassed.*

MAGGIE. 'Elen, I need to go home and wash. I'm pure bowfin.

CATHIE. A hot cup o' tea's what I need.

MAGGIE. I cannae believe I'm gonnae miss *Dallas* the night.

WORKER. I've no gone a week without looking at Bobby Ewing's face since November.

CATHIE. I'm cold to my bones.

MAGGIE. How many times is my mammy expected to come up wi' warm tea?

WORKER 2. Least your mammy didnae bring a leccy bill wi' your flask. This needs paid, 'Elen.

WORKER. When are we getting strike pay?

CATHIE. I heard the treasurer fae Lithgows Shipyard came round wi' money from their kitty.

HELEN. Aye. My man's cousin, Patrick, came wi' him. One a the workers heard what was happening.

MAGGIE. Thanks to STV!

HELEN. Heard it on his car radio in fact. Finance committee can sort bills that need sorting. Speak to Bridie Groenewald.

FINLAY. How much are Lithgows giving us?

HELEN. More than we could a hoped for.

CATHIE. Ten pence a head? Fifteen?

HELEN. Fifty pence a head. And they had enough in their kitty to gi' it us ahead a time.

FINLAY. Good on Lithgows for delivering for us.

WORKER. Can they pay my leccy bill an' all?

HELEN. Emergencies first. Wi' two hundred and forty leccy bills to pay, we'll burn through Lithgows' fifty pences in nae time.

MAGGIE. What about the semiconductors next door?

FINLAY. I don't think they'll gi' us fifty pence a head but mebbe five?

HELEN. Nothing fae them. Not a single fivepence nor any solidarity. They're keeping their heads down.

MAGGIE. We see them every day!

CATHIE. Least they could do is lend us an urn or two.

IIELEN. How are we gonnae get an urn through they bars?

CATHIE. Kitchen's just there, taunting us.

MAGGIE. You need to get the key off management, 'Elen.

CATHIE. For the kitchen or for the front door?

MAGGIE. Both.

HELEN. How are we gonnae persuade management to gi' us any keys?

CATHIE. Our machine-maintenance man could claim spousal privilege. He's married to a supervisor sitting on the other side a the barricade.

MAGGIE. Alec can get the front-door key. You need to make him, 'Elen.

CATHIE. Speak to Alec.

Clutching at Straws

ALEC. Greta'll no gi' me the front-door key, 'Elen. She could lose her job.

HELEN. She's gonnae lose her job if they ship all this off to Northern Ireland. I cannae see youse living in a war zone like Derry.

ALEC. I'm telling you, she'll no let that key leave her office.

HELEN. Mebbe it disnae need to? All we need is the shape a the key. Locksmiths can do the rest. A bar a soap would take its shape.

ALEC. Do I look like John Steed out a *The Avengers*? Did somebody put a bowler hat on my head and gi' me an umbrella without me looking?

HELEN. No. And I'm no Emma Peel. I'm sorry, Alec. Clutching at straws here.

Same Rule for Everybody

FINLAY. Mammy, can I have a word?

HELEN. What's on your mind, son?

FINLAY. I'm due at college on Monday. My exams are no long away. I'm part a this. I'll no let anybody down. I just… What do I say to college? How long will I be off?

HELEN. I don't know how to answer that, son. I've no heard

whether our union's gonnae back us. If I had a working phone I could start getting some answers.

FINLAY. I only need out for a couple a hours each day to keep up wi' college. If you let me slip out the way Maggie did.

WORKER 2. Let me slip out an' all. I'll get supplies for everybody.

WORKER. If you let me, I'll bring shortbread.

CATHIE. Can you bring an urn?

WORKER. And a telly!

HELEN. The polis let Maggie back in that first night but this isnae our property. If you're caught climbing over the roof, management will call it breaking in and this whole thing will be over. Naebody's going out that window.

FINLAY. But what about college?

HELEN. I said naebody!

FINLAY. Right.

He walks away, despondent. HELEN *follows after.*

HELEN. Finlay lad. I'm sorry. It's got to be the same rule for everybody. If I could just get a working phone.

MAGGIE. I've got us one!

HELEN. No now, Maggie.

MAGGIE. I've got us a phone.

CATHIE. You mean two tin cans attached to a piece a string?

MAGGIE. We've got the internal extension phone, right, that can take calls from management but that disnae phone out. So I've rewired it wi' the wire for the payphone that does, see?

CATHIE. You couldnae rewire a coathanger!

MAGGIE. I followed the wire fae the payphone, climbed onto the roof and marked it on the big box up there. Then I followed the wire fae the extension phone and I swapped the two wires over.

HELEN. Will that work?

MAGGIE. I'm gonnae try now.

All the noise stops. They all crowd round the extension phone.

There's a dial tone.

FINLAY. Maggie Wallace, you're a genius, isn't she, Mammy?

HELEN. It's gonnae make life easier, for sure.

MAGGIE. Who'd you need to call first, 'Elen?

HELEN. You make the first call. It's your handiwork. Phone your mammy.

MAGGIE. You sure?

CATHIE. I'll phone her if you don't.

MAGGIE. I'm phoning!

MAGGIE dials her mammy's number.

Mammy? It's me, Maggie. I managed to rewire the phone so…

CATHIE. What's wrang?

MAGGIE. The pips went. And there's no hole to put in my two pence. I'm sorry, 'Elen.

HELEN walks away, disappointed. MAGGIE is crestfallen.

CATHIE. I knew it wouldnae work. Nothing you do ever works out right.

Moon the Loon

MAGGIE. Alright, Jimmy? You hiding out here an' all?

FINLAY becomes JIMMY. He's not in a good way but he tries his best for MAGGIE.

JIMMY. Alright, Maggie.

MAGGIE. You're sweating like a turkey at Christmas.

JIMMY. Feel like Keith Moon didnae go to heaven. He's sitting behind my ribs thumping one thousand beats a minute. Don't laugh.

MAGGIE. It's a funny image. Moon the Loon thrashing about in your ribcage. Is Pete Townshend in there wi' him?

JIMMY. I feel rotten, Maggie. Got this sense a dread – I need out. I need some fresh air.

MAGGIE. You need a drink, you mean?

None a us is going anywhere, Jimmy. You just need to put your mind to something.

JIMMY. What? There's nothing to do!

MAGGIE. I know that. That's how come I ended up on the roof, making a fool out a mysel.

Tell me about that cruise you're always going on about.

JIMMY. When I've saved up the money, I'm gonnae get mysel down to Southampton to get on the SS *Canberra*. There's a massive dance flair and a swimming pool and a cinema wi' stereophonic sound.

MAGGIE. Stereophonic sound, eh?

JIMMY. I'm going to go all-out on one a they cabins that has a fridge and a cocktail cabinet and a telly. Mebbe you could come wi' us?

MAGGIE. You can be the one to tell my mammy. You mind what she was like when you called the house that time.

JIMMY. Aye, she gied me about as much time as you'd gi' a cat at a dog show.

MAGGIE. My brother'd gi' you even less.

JIMMY. That's a pure shame.

You're magic, you know that, Maggie Wallace.

MAGGIE. How?

JIMMY. You know exactly what to do and say to make things right.

MAGGIE. Try telling my sister that.

JIMMY. I'm telling you.

Something could happen between them here but they are interrupted by a knocking.

Negotiation

HELEN (*to us*). Wee Bob Charters is knocking on every window shouting at folk to get off the factory flair. The American owners are breathing down his neck about making sure nae damage is done to the equipment and fabric.

(*To* BOB CHARTERS.) They're just stretching their legs.

BOB CHARTERS. Well I'd appreciate it if you could keep them inside the canteen.

HELEN. Well I'd appreciate it if you gied me the key to the kitchen.

BOB CHARTERS. This isn't a negotiation.

HELEN. No. If it was a negotiation, I'd be asking you for a working phone.

BOB CHARTERS. I could get that payphone working for you again.

HELEN. Could you?

BOB CHARTERS. Of course. If you move the chairs and give me access to the factory.

HELEN. Very funny.

BOB CHARTERS. No phone then.

HELEN. No keeping my lot off the factory flair then. Have fun telling the American owners.

BOB CHARTERS. Helen…

HELEN. Look, I'm no trying to negotiate but we've no had a cup a tea or anything. It'd make it easier to keep everybody in the canteen and off the factory flair if we all had a wee cup a tea to drink.

BOB CHARTERS.…Aye. Okay. I'll get you the kitchen key.

Be More Than You Think You Are

HELEN (*to the workers*). Kitchen's open. Now we can really get cooking.

(*To us.*) Alec, can I have a word.

ALEC. How did you persuade Charters to open the kitchen?

HELEN. I don't know, Alec. But now I'm questioning everything. Hiding away in here all polite waiting for they Americans to see sense, hoping our union'll see fit to back us eventually – I'm no sure that's gonnae work. Mebbe Maggie had it right that first night wi' STV? I hate cameras and fuss but now I'm thinking if we're gonnae win this thing, I'm gonnae have to get out that door and make some noise. Be more than I think I am. But I cannae do that unless you decide to be more than you think you are too. What do you say? Mebbe it's time to reach for that bowler hat and umbrella and find your inner hero?

(*To us.*) 'John Steed' got us our front-door key.

Mebbe he footered around wi' a bar a soap to get us it or mebbe Greta just gied him it – she's a Greenock girl after all, management or no. But either way, it changed things for us. We set up a shift system.

CATHIE. Eight till eight, wi' rotas for cooking and cleaning.

FINLAY. And maintaining the machinery.

HELEN. When their chores are done, the women sit about chatting and playing cards.

MAGGIE. A lot of us knit.

CATHIE. You never. You just work your way round the line asking folk if you're doing it right. You're all 'Ina, I don't think I'm doing it right.' So Ina knits you a few rows and passes it back, then you ask the next person who knits you a few more rows and the next person.

MAGGIE. Got a whole damn scarf made without knitting a single row!

HELEN. Our biggest men stand on the doors checking bags as workers leave so naebody'll be tempted to take the thousands a pounds' worth a denim for a walk.

And I… I get mysel in front a they cameras.

Girls on Film

In the original production, Duran Duran's 'Girls on Film' acted as a holding form for the ensuing scenes, starting with the iconic camera-shutter intro. With or without the music, the following short scenes should come thick and fast. HELEN can be almost dizzy with moving from the journalists into mini-scenes and back again.

The ensemble hold up wee beginnings of knitted sweaters which, put together, read: 'ONE WEEK IN'.

JOURNALIST. Is this a militant campaign?

HELEN. All we want is they American managers to sit down wi' us and agree a deal to keep our jobs.

JOURNALIST. You're one week into this occupation – have you got the backing of your union yet?

HELEN. No but we've got lots a support locally. We're getting more support every single day.

JOURNALIST. What do your son and daughter working at the factory think of all this – can we speak to them?

FINLAY (*quietly to* HELEN). I don't mind talking to them, Mammy.

HELEN. I know what I'm doing and if I never work again, that is what it is, but I don't want all this to harm you. Don't you be talking to anybody, you hear?

FINLAY. Aye, okay.

HELEN (*to the* JOURNALIST). Anything you need to ask, you can ask me.

The ensemble hold up their knitting. The sweaters are taking shape. They read: 'TWO WEEKS IN'.

JOURNALIST. Is it true you were wolf-whistled at and catcalled at the meeting of Pipefitters' Shop Stewards?

HELEN. I don't want to – I don't think we need to –

JOURNALIST. Is it true?

HELEN is back in that meeting, standing in front of all the men.

HECKLER. Speak up, love!

HECKLER 2. Get a lung full a air in your chest.

HECKLER 3. What you talking about her chest for?

HELEN. We need to make a stand – the VF Corporation are talking about the value a the pound but it's a /

Somebody wolf-whistles. HELEN is disconcerted.

It's a… an excuse. They've used local money to keep their costs down and now /

More whistling and whoops.

They're looking for a way to… to… to… /

HELEN cannot be heard above the wolf-whistles.

Mebbe there was a wee bit a wolf-whistling. But I delivered,

didn't I? I came away wi' my donation buckets so full
I needed help getting them back to the factory.

MAGGIE. Took Theresa Houston the best part of an hour to
count the cash!

HELEN. Worth a bit a wolf-whistling that, I'd say.

JOURNALIST. How are you going to strike a deal with the
Americans if you're spending all your time begging for
money?

HELEN. I've a good team going out for me. You get a sense a
who you can trust to do it.

MAGGIE. Cath'rine Robertson was the first one she picked.

HELEN. And they're no begging. They're explaining our fight
to folk who want to support us.

MAGGIE. I'm happy for Cath'rine.

FINLAY. You seem it.

MAGGIE. We've all got our strengths. Mine is raising morale.
Singing and entertaining folk.

CATHIE. How's that *your* strength? Cath'rine's the club singer.

MAGGIE. Aye but even Cath'rine agrees I do the best
impressions. My Gladys is *Hi De Hi*-larious!

MAGGIE *plays the distinctive three notes on the xylophone
from Gladys's* Hi-de-Hi! *announcements.*

'Hello, campers!'

JOURNALIST. What are you doing with the money you're
raising, Mrs Monaghan?

HELEN. We've set up a finance committee. We're giving it to
those who need it most. I've whole families relying on the
wages from our factory.

JOURNALIST. You're three weeks in now and still no strike
pay from your union?

HELEN. No – No yet – but – We're hopeful we'll get their
support.

*The ensemble hold up their finished jumpers, which read:
'ONE MONTH IN'.*

JOURNALIST. Who's been your most high-profile visiter?

HELEN. James Milne, General Secretary a the Scottish Trades
Union. Jimmy Airlie and Jimmy Reid, who had a thing or
two to say about occupying their place a work. We're getting
support fae all sorts a folk.

FINLAY. Ma, this woman's come fae Liverpool wanting to talk
to you. From an organisation called /

LIVERPUDLIAN. Big Flame. We provide a political focus
for workers involved in single-issue campaigns who share
our perspective. The capitalist system exploits misogyny as
a means to divide the proletariat into subdivisions. They fear
our strength if we resist this oppression to find working-class
solidarity.

FINLAY. She's a… communist.

LIVERPUDLIAN. We actually place ourselves between the red
and the green. Between communism and /

HELEN (*to* FINLAY) It's no the back a eight already? I'll need
to go down and get your daddy's tea.

(*To the* LIVERPUDLIAN.) Sorry, you were saying – you
place yoursel between communism and…?

LIVERPUDLIAN (*unimpressed*). Feminism.

HELEN (*to the* JOURNALIST). Who we are disnae always
match what folk want us to be. We've to stay focused on our
own agenda. Getting our jobs back.

*The ensemble hold up multiple knitted jumpers, which read:
'SIX WEEKS IN'.*

JOURNALIST. Is it true the leader of the opposition is planning
to pay you a visit?

MAGGIE. Ellen, they semiconductor lot are in our car park
again even though we've telt them we're needing every
space for Michael Foot's visit. Me and some a the others
thought we could let down their tyres – teach them a lesson.

HELEN. Wi' all they cameras here filming us? Don't you dare. What's up wi' your face?

MAGGIE. I told Annemarie White to bring in her sunlamp. The young ones are wanting a tan to look good for the cameras.

HELEN. You should knock stupid ideas like that on the head, Maggie, no entertain them.

CATHIE. Folk have taken to calling the lot a you the Dirty Dozen. And everybody knows it's you that's the bad influence.

Look at the state a you!

MAGGIE. How, am I a wee bit red?

CATHIE. A wee bit? If there was a bull in here, he'd head straight for you.

MAGGIE. I didnae stay on it as long as Annemarie White.

FINLAY. She's at the hospital wi' third-degree burns. There's nothing white about Annemarie White the noo.

HELEN (*to the* JOURNALIST). Aye, Michael Foot's people have been in touch. We're looking forward to welcoming him.

JOURNALIST. And still nothing from your union?

HELEN. We're still waiting to /

JOURNALIST. It's been five weeks.

HELEN. Well, I –

JOURNALIST. How do you expect the world to take you seriously when your own union doesn't?

HELEN. I don't think they –

JOURNALIST. Are you ever going to get an answer, Mrs Monaghan?

HELEN. I'll get an answer. I will. Even if I have to go to London to get one.

London.

MR SMITH. Thanks for coming all this way. I got a bottle of whisky in especially for you.

HELEN. Did you, aye?

MR SMITH. Make you feel at home after the long journey down.

HELEN. No for me, ta.

MR SMITH. Your union rep tells me we've met before?

HELEN. About a year ago, long before I knew we had trouble at our factory, I came down for a meeting where you were speaking about the need to fight against job losses.

MR SMITH. Well, I'm sorry my words proved so prescient.

HELEN. I don't need sorries – what I need from you, as the General Secretary a the Tailors and Garment's Union is a commitment to support our fight.

MR SMITH. You don't mince your words, do you, Mrs Monaghan?

HELEN. I don't have time. Redundancy day is April 30th. Last six weeks I've been fighting wi' no a penny in strike pay fae my union and now I've only six more weeks before redundancy day lands and we lose all two hundred and forty jobs. If you're gonnae support us, now's the time, Mr Smith.

MR SMITH. It's no small thing to occupy a factory you don't own, Mrs Monaghan. We're still exploring the legality of the situation with our lawyers. I know you want our backing but you may have to make some concessions.

HELEN. Concessions?

MR SMITH. We would be more confident about our legal position if you were outside the factory. One proposal is that we set you up with a caravan.

HELEN. A caravan?!

MR SMITH. With a view of the entrance to the factory.

HELEN. So we can watch they Americans at VF Corporation walk away wi' our machinery?

MR SMITH. You would continue to picket the door, obviously. Just from the outside.

HELEN. From a position a weakness?

MR SMITH. From a position of safety, in a legal sense.

HELEN. Can you show me the letters?

MR SMITH. Sorry?

HELEN. The letters between you and your lawyers about the legality of our occupation.

MR SMITH. I… That's… Well, I… I hope you're not suggesting there is no such correspondence?

HELEN. I'm just asking to see it. I want to see where it says what we're doing is illegal.

MR SMITH. We're still exploring the issue.

HELEN. Aye and while you explore the issue, it's local men and women have been keeping us going. We've had shipyard men gi' money off their salaries when they're already working reduced hours. We've had meat fae the butchers, veg deliveries, camp beds and blankets, boxes a booze I'll no let any a my lot touch until we win this thing. We've had nothing from the fence-sitters who work at the semiconductor plant next door to us but we've had the BT Union put in a phone in its own shed at the top a the hill near the factory so I can keep pestering you and we've had folk from Bathgate to Burnley to Bristol sending us letters a support wi' all the coin they can spare. Saving these jobs means something to all a them – they're standing wi' us, delivering for us. Meanwhile the National Union a Tailors and Garment Workers, *our* union, have offered nothing.

MR SMITH. Not nothing /

HELEN. / No, you're right. I had to travel five hundred miles to get it but today you've offered something. A caravan.

MR SMITH. Mrs Monagan /

HELEN. I just want your support, Mr Smith.

MR SMITH. I can't give it. Not without some concessions.

HELEN. You banged your fists. At that conference. Wi' all the Tailors and Garment Unions gathered. You were shouting and bawling and banging your fists against the table saying how we've got to do something about job losses. What exactly are you doing about it? 'Cause I'm doing something about it but I need your support. Or is banging on tables all you've got to offer?

(*To the* JOURNALISTS.) I'm pleased to be able to report that our strike has, as of today, been formally recognised and endorsed by the National Union of Tailors and Garment Workers.

New jumpers are held up with images of spring (daffodils and crocuses) on them; they read: 'EIGHT WEEKS IN'.

A Bonfire

FINLAY *passes* HELEN *a white envelope.*

HELEN. What's this?

FINLAY. It's long and white so I reckon it's your redundancy offer. Found it unopened in a drawer at home.

HELEN. Aye and that's where it can stay.

FINLAY. Everybody's got theirs now. Thought mebbe we could do something thegither. Make a grand statement.

HELEN. Like what?

FINLAY. A bonfire, I thought. There's a metal drum we could use out the back.

CATHIE. Can we, 'Elen?

HELEN. Aye. Okay. Let's do that.

WORKER. How much is yours for, 'Elen?

CATHIE. Mine's three hundred and fifty pounds.

FINLAY. Two hundred pounds.

WORKER. Four hundred pounds. I've worked here longer than
    you.

CATHIE. I could really do wi' that money.

WORKER 2. Tore mine up the moment I realised what it was.

HELEN. Aye. Mine got shoved in the drawer, same reason.

CATHIE. Are you no gonnae open it?

WORKER. You've worked here longest. Could be a lot. Might
    as well see the number before you burn it.

HELEN. I wouldnae sell my job for any amount a money. It
    makes nae difference what they're (offering) –

    HELEN *stops short seeing the number in the now opened
    letter.*

CATHIE. How much is it for?

HELEN. A thousand.

FINLAY. A thousand pounds's a lot a money.

HELEN. Aye.

MAGGIE (*breaking out of the scene*). I don't remember this bit.
    I don't think I was there.

CATHIE. Aye you were. We dragged in that metal drum, stuffed
    it wi' old cardboard and lighter fluid. Cath'rine Robertson
    sang 'Links on the Chain'. She'd changed the words to fit,
    wrote them on the wall.

    '*It started off in Greenock, it's where we make Lee Jeans.
    The factory is closing, no jobs for us it seems.*'

MAGGIE. I remember the song but I definitely wisnae there
    for the letters. What was I doing? Getting pissed off wi' they
    semiconductor cars in our car park probably.

HELEN (*distracted by the letter*). You leave they semiconductor
    lot to me, Maggie.

MAGGIE. I'm just wanting to do something useful.

HELEN. Stick wi' singing songs and that Geordie impression
you do.

MAGGIE. It isnae Geordie, it's Welsh!

I mind where I was. I was wi' the one person who made me
feel listened to. I was wi' /

ALL. / Jimmy.

MAGGIE. Gi' us that flask please, Jimmy.

FINLAY *becomes a very drunk* JIMMY.

JIMMY. I'd gi' you anything, Maggie.

MAGGIE. We need to get some tea down you.

JIMMY. You're a beautiful human, you know that, Maggie
Wallace.

MAGGIE. That's nice a you, Jimmy. But you need to sober up
or you're gonnae be in more hot water than this teabag. Here
you go, get it drank.

JIMMY. I mean it about that cruise, Maggie. I'd like to go wi'
you. I know I'm always bending your ear about my ex and
my kids. But it's just 'cause I like talking to you. Better than
anybody else.

MAGGIE. I like talking to you too, Jimmy. When you're
no pickled like an onion. You make me feel like I've got
something to offer. Like my opinion counts.

JIMMY. Your opinion counts, Maggie.

MAGGIE. It disnae, Jimmy. No really.

JIMMY. What about all they young ones? They look up to you.

MAGGIE. They shouldnae. All we do is mess about. You know
what they call us? The Dirty Dozen. Cath'rine is out there
making hersel' useful and I'm in here, the butt a everybody's
joke.

JIMMY. Your opinion is beautiful, Maggie.

JIMMY *tries to get up and stumbles over, making a racket. The ensemble, who have been building the fire, all look over.*

MAGGIE. Jimmy! You cannae let her see you like this.

But it's too late…

HELEN. Oh Jimmy… what did I tell you about the booze?

JIMMY. I'm sorry, 'Elen.

HELEN. You know what I'm gonnae say.

JIMMY. Aye. I cannae be here.

HELEN. No wi' drink in you. They're all out there building a fire to burn their redundancy offers. And once they're ash, that's us without any exit route. All eyes on us. The polis outside just waiting. The managers just waiting.

MAGGIE. He'll no drink here again, 'Elen. Will you, Jimmy? You'll make sure you're sober when you're here, right?

HELEN. It's too late for that.

MAGGIE. I'll make sure he disnae drink again. You can trust me, 'Elen. I'll make sure this is the last time. Gi' him a chance, please. This is Jimmy we're talking about. He's learned your son all he knows in the job.

HELEN. You're no making this any easier, Maggie.

Beat.

This is the end a the line for you, Jimmy. I'm sorry.

MAGGIE. Finlay'll have something to say about you doing this.

Beat.

JIMMY (*suddenly sober*). No, he'll no. No if I've learnt him anything, he'll no. I always tell him a good mechanic coming to a broken machine does one thing before he does anything else – he looks at the big picture. And that's all Finlay's mammy's doing the now.

Good luck wi' it, 'Elen. You'll show them, I know you will.

JIMMY *exits, dignified.*

MAGGIE. You didnae need to do that. He listens to me. You could have trusted me to make sure he was okay.

HELEN. Trusted you? All you do is mess around, Maggie. You and the Dirty Dozen. Keeping folk up at night wi' your nonsense. Climbing onto the roof to smoke your fags. Sneaking out on the night shift for a pint.

MAGGIE. I only do that 'cause that's what you expect a me. Why did you never ask me to go out collecting? I mind when Cath'rine came back fae speaking at Glasgow Uni she seemed different. Taller. She couldnae believe they academic types were listening to her, a wee lassie. Said the sense a pride made her chest go out like a pigeon. Like one a my daddy's doos. How'd you never ask me to do that? Mebbe I would do more if you expected more.

HELEN. You want to talk about what folk expect? What about you? All a you. Expecting me to get us through this, to win it, to make it all alright again. You're all like weans – expecting Mammy to sort it all out wi' no clue what's going on out there. What if we lose the jobs and the redundancy money? What then? Even if there were any jobs going, what employer's gonnae jump at taking on anybody militant enough to take part in a failed occupation? When women come to me and tell me they cannae stick it, the rest a you look like thunder but part a me is glad. It's one less body to worry about. One less lassie relying on me. 'Cause redundancy day is coming at us fast and I don't know if I can make it right. And the weight a you all is too much, Maggie Wallace. You think I should expect more a you, well I'm sorry, I'm too busy dealing wi' what you all expect a me.

FINLAY. Fire's ready, Mammy.

HELEN *is embarrassed that she's allowed herself to share so much. She collects herself.*

HELEN. Aye. You coming, Maggie? I know you're angry but /

MAGGIE. I don't feel angry, 'Elen. I feel flat.

(*Threatening…*) Like a tyre that's had its air let out.

HELEN. No, Maggie.

Maggie, if you let those tyres down, I'll have to let you go an' all. You know that, Maggie. Please. Maggie!

MAGGIE*'s gone.* HELEN *looks to* FINLAY.

HELEN. Don't ask. Come on then. Let's get these letters burnt.

In the original production, the company sang 'Links on the Chain' by Phil Ochs, with the lyrics the workers had reworked: 'Eight weeks ago we occupied the fuckin' factory flair. We barricaded the bosses in, and they're still fuckin' there.'

HELEN *walks to the raging fire. One by one, the ensemble throw in their letters. It's* HELEN*'s turn. She looks over at* MAGGIE, *who joins them, a look of mischief in her eye.*

HELEN *throws her letter in.* MAGGIE *has joined now and, looking right at* HELEN, *pours petrol on the flames. The flames surge.*

Interval.

Ghost Town

In the original production, the ensemble greeted us back after the interval with a much bleaker sound, the haunting 'Ghost Town' by The Specials.

WORKER. Did you hear?

WORKER 2. About Linwood car plant?

WORKER. The most militant factory in Scotland.

WORKER 3. They're giving up.

WORKER 4. Four thousand, eight hundred employees.

WORKER 2. All out on the street, looking for work.

WORKER 3. If they cannae make it work, we don't stand a chance.

MAGGIE. Cheer up, 'Elen. It might never happen.

HELEN. It just did. Linwood car plant closed. You should try turning on the news once in a while.

MAGGIE. Too depressing.

HELEN. You got that right. That boy starving himself over in Northern Ireland. Standing up to Thatcher the only way he can, by no eating. He started the month after we started here. Sixty days he's been at it. They think he'll be dead within the week, unless he gi'es up. All I can think is how lonely he must feel. So very lonely.

MAGGIE. What's it got to do wi' us?

HELEN. Bobby Sands?

MAGGIE. Linwood?

HELEN. You must have heard what they're all saying. If they cannae make it work…

MAGGIE. Naw, that's no right. They're nothing to do wi' us. They don't have our secret weapon. They don't have you.

You wanted to see me.

HELEN. Aye.

What did I say I'd do if you let down the tyres?

MAGGIE. They semiconductor workers are scabs. They've no gied us a penny /

HELEN. What did I say?

MAGGIE. How many times have we told them no to park /

HELEN. Maggie!

MAGGIE. You said you'd put me out.

HELEN. I had to lie to the polis for you.

Beat.

You're done here.

MAGGIE. But –

I've been here since I was sixteen. You helped me back at the beginning when I was learning the job.

HELEN. I did.

MAGGIE. I've been fighting this wi' you all since January. We're nearly at our ninety days. Redundancy day. We've had that many dropouts, you need me. We've already lost nearly a hundred. You cannae kick me out when /

HELEN. We're done, Maggie.

I've put in a long shift and now I'm going home. You need to get your things thegither and say your goodbyes. You'll no be coming back to this factory.

MAGGIE.…Fine.

At HELEN*'s home…*

FINLAY SENIOR. You're fed up, Finlay lad. How do you think I feel? It's my wage that's paying for her to get her buses and trains all around the place. Your mammy brings in buckets full a cash and she'll no let one penny a that money come back to us.

FINLAY. There's folk wi' no wages coming into their homes.

FINLAY SENIOR. And it's right they should be looked after but she thought this'd be over weeks ago. And then there's the elephant in the room. She'll no let me ask the question but you know and I know /

FINLAY. / There's a chance we're doing all this for nothing.

Sitting around waitin' for them to drag us out when our ninety-day redundancy is done. And we'll have nothing to show for it.

HELEN (*to us*). My son and my man saying all the stuff I'm carrying heavy in my heart. You'd think I'd be relieved to hear them say it, to share all that worry thegither. To have it out in the open.

I wisnae relieved. I was gutted.

FINLAY SENIOR. You're home! Your tea's on the cooker. It's mince and totties again but I'm definitely getting better at it. Tasted as good as yours, didn't it, son?

FINLAY. I'd no go that far.

HELEN. I'm just home to put a washing on.

FINLAY SENIOR. Difficult day?

HELEN *plonks a soap powder box in front of* FINLAY SENIOR.

FINLAY SENIOR. What's this for?

HELEN. There's a promotion for free train rides. I'll cut these out and then it'll no be your wage that pays for my meetings.

FINLAY SENIOR. You heard that, aye?

Sit down, the clothes can wait. You've a letter. I'll make you some tea.

HELEN. I've lost my appetite. I'm gonnae head back to the factory.

FINLAY. To do a double shift? You're just back.

HELEN. I need to be wi' folk who believe in what we're doing. If there are any left.

Enjoy the View

FINLAY SENIOR *joins* HELEN *on the roof of the factory.*

FINLAY SENIOR. Mind if I join you? When Finlay couldnae find you down there, he thought you must have gone AWOL. Luckily one a the lassies seen you climbing up here.

HELEN. Never been before. It's Maggie Wallace's spot. She and her Dirty Dozen smoke their fags up here. Or she did. Before I sent her away.

FINLAY SENIOR. I'm guessing you're hiding unless my wife's suddenly taken up smoking?

HELEN. Hardly hiding when I told folk how to get hold a me, if they need me.

She holds up a CB radio.

Bridie Groenewald's son gied us it. It's a CB radio.

FINLAY SENIOR. What's that for?

HELEN. Nae clue. He seems to think we can make some use a it beyond playing walkie-talkies.

(*Talking into it.*) 'Elen Monaghan is not AWOL. 'Elen is on the roof. Over and out.

CB RADIO (*static*). Enjoy the view.

FINLAY SENIOR. It is a decent view.

HELEN. Aye. Greenock's no bad fae up here. Twinkly. It's just on the ground it's all falling to pieces.

I've been sitting here thinking about my job.

FINLAY SENIOR. Running all this?

HELEN. My real job. Quality control. When you see a pair
   a jeans and they've no been sewed right, you're no wanting
   to speak to the girl who sewed it, you just have to. And
   when a wee girl is sacked before she's been gied a chance to
   succeed, you're no wanting to make a fuss wi' management.
   You just have to.

I'm no choosing all this, you know. It chose me.

FINLAY SENIOR. I know, love.

HELEN. I keep thinking I'll just do what I'm doing until
   somebody calls time on it but I'm starting to worry that…

FINLAY SENIOR. That you're the one who has to call time on
   it?

HELEN. I don't know how to do that. That's no for me. No
   matter how much I'm wanting done wi' it. I just cannae be
   the one to –

I cannae.

Beat.

But if you want to make that decision for me…

FINLAY SENIOR. I cannae make that decision for you.

HELEN. No even if I want you to?

FINLAY SENIOR. You're wanting me to start throwing my
   weight around? Should I be screaming and shouting and
   telling you 'Woman, this has to stop!' That what you're
   wanting?

HELEN. Mebbe.

FINLAY SENIOR. You're the only one who can say when it's
   time for this to stop, my love.

HELEN. I know.

She passes him the letter.

FINLAY SENIOR. This the letter that came for you?

HELEN. Aye, it's a leccy bill.

FINLAY SENIOR. I've paid our leccy bill.

HELEN. It's no for home. It's for here. For the factory. And it's in my name.

FINLAY SENIOR. They cannae do that, can they? How much is it for?

HELEN. Four thousand pound. I've never seen four thousand pound in my life.

FINLAY SENIOR. We cannae pay that. What happens when we don't pay that?

HELEN. I don't know. I've nae answers left.

FINLAY SENIOR.… This could be your way out, love? They workers down there would understand that the owners have you over a barrel. Playing dirty like this. This would be them ending it. No you.

HELEN. Aye. Mebbe.

FINLAY SENIOR. Whatever you decide is alright by me.

Beat.

But either way, can we get off this roof 'cause if I stay sitting on this icy concrete much longer I'll need a crowbar to unstick mysel.

HELEN. Aye, we'll go down. You should head on home.

FINLAY SENIOR. You no coming wi' me?

HELEN. I've some thinking to do.

Ending It

HELEN *'s in the factory now when* MAGGIE *appears.*

HELEN. If you're wanting to see your wee Dirty Dozen pals,

you'll have to see them somewhere else. You're no part a this now, Maggie Wallace.

MAGGIE. I came to speak to you.

HELEN. What is there to say?

MAGGIE. I've been thinking a lot and I shouldn't a waited for you to expect more a me. I should a proved to you I could do more. I think I still can, if you'll gi' me the chance. Let me speak out for us, the way Cath'rine does.

A commotion.

Let me show you I can do it. I know I can / prove it to you if you just…

HELEN. / Something's kicking off. Finlay, son, what's happening?

FINLAY (*real urgency*). Mammy, you need to get out a here. The building's on fire. Greta's calling the fire service.

HELEN. You're joking?

FINLAY. Do I look like I'm joking? We need to get everybody out.

MAGGIE. And hand the place back to the Americans on a platter? Management'll be thanking their lucky stars.

FINLAY. Luck? I'm no sure luck has much to do wi' it. Who do you think lit the fire?

HELEN. They wouldnae.

FINLAY. We think they've stuffed paper in the vents.

CATHIE. What good will a burnt-down factory do them?

HELEN. Vents are flameproof. The place'll no burn. They're trying to smoke us out. They're throwing everything they got at us now. Is the fire contained?

FINLAY. Aye. It's in the vents and the mechanics are dealing wi' it but the smoke's dangerous enough.

MAGGIE. What do you want to do, 'Elen?

CATHIE. Did you no hear him say the word 'dangerous'? We need to get out a here.

HELEN. We could open all the windows? It's no ideal but if we leave, we're letting them end it. And mebbe that's right. Mebbe it's time I face up to the elephant in the room. Mebbe that's what youse all want?

Finlay, son, is that what you want?

Now's the time to say it if it is. Say it to my face.

Beat.

FINLAY. No, Mammy. That's no what I want.

Is it what you want?

Beat. HELEN *considers. This is it, the moment of no return.*

HELEN. Naw. Naw, it's no.

FINLAY. What are you thinking?

HELEN. I'm thinking this isnae them ending it. This is them starting it. I was getting tired but now I'm angry.

FINLAY. Me an' all.

HELEN. This thing disnae end till I say it does.

FINLAY. Too right.

HELEN. Anybody who wants to go, can. But me and my boy, we're staying.

CATHIE. Aye I'll stay an' all. But you'll have to stick up for me if my mammy takes one one sniff a my clothes and wants to skelp me for smoking.

MAGGIE. I'm wanting to stay. If you'll have me back?

HELEN. There's an SNP conference up in Aberdeeen next month. Lots a influential folk there. And film cameras. If we make it through redundancy day, you can speak at that.

MAGGIE. Aye. I can do that.

HELEN. And in the meantime, we need to get ahead a they Americans. I'm done wi' being blindsided by them. We need to make better use a the CB radios. Get eyes out on the road.

MAGGIE (*still worrying over the conference*). Did you say film cameras? At the conference.

HELEN. Are you getting cold feet?

MAGGIE. No, I can do it. Definitely. You can trust me.

HELEN. Seems only fair to trust you when you are putting your trust in me.

MAGGIE. Hell, 'Elen, I trust you so much I'd let you pack my parachute.

FINLAY. I think we all feel like that, Mammy. If you say jump, we'll jump.

HELEN. I'm no wanting you to jump.

CATHIE. What are you wanting us to do?

HELEN. Just keep standing.

In the original production the actors sang Joe Dolce's 'Shaddap You Face' with rewritten lyrics: 'Don't shuttupatheplace!'

Redundancy Day

The ensemble unravel a long, long scarf. It reads: 'TWELVE WEEKS IN: REDUNDANCY DAY'.

CATHIE. What's wi' the singalong?

MAGGIE. Redundancy day officially started eight hours ago and I've done every single thing on 'Elen's list and so all that's left is to keep up morale.

CATHIE. Morale? This isnae the trenches, Maggie.

MAGGIE. Tell your face that.

CATHIE. I didnae sleep much last night.

MAGGIE. You have a hard night working on a rota, aye?

CATHIE. They're no as easy as you think, Maggie. Everybody's got something you need to work round and you finally think you've got it sorted and then somebody's sick or 'Elen sends them out collecting so you're back to the drawing board trying to fill their place but you know that Sandra cannae take it on 'cause her wean has her asthma clinic on a Wednesday and Wendy looks after her mammy that day and Trisha could have covered but she's already done a double shift so she could take the night off for her man's birthday. It's complicated!

MAGGIE. Aye well it wisnae all singing and dancing here. Naebody got a wink.

CATHIE. How?

MAGGIE. Bridie Groenewald's son gied us a warning at two a.m. on the radio that there were trucks heading our way.

CATHIE. They Americans sending in the heavies?

MAGGIE. We thought it might be. 'Elen was standing there in her goonie saying the heavies would just have to wait for her to get dressed before they marched her out. But it was a false alarm.

CATHIE. Does 'Elen really think they'll send in the heavies the day?

MAGGIE. She's no saying much at all.

CATHIE. Typical if it all ends the day.

MAGGIE. How?

CATHIE. My man's never stopped giving me a hard time for being here twelve hours a day and having nae money to do anything when I am wi' him.

MAGGIE. Where's his sense a solidarity? Weasly wee wimp.

CATHIE. Aye well it's over wi' him and me now just in time for us getting kicked out a here. Typical.

MAGGIE. Are you gonnae greet about him?

CATHIE. No here I'm no.

MAGGIE. Good.

CATHIE. How? 'Cause I'd embarrass you?

MAGGIE. Naw. 'Cause he never deserved your Farrah Fawcett curls. He's was like a low-budget Charlie – telling you what to do and never really there when you needed him. He's the one who should be crying 'cause he's the one who's lost an angel.

CATHIE. Thanks, Maggie.

FINLAY. Did I just hear the Wallace sisters having a wee moment?

CATHIE. At least we can end one thing on a positive note.

FINLAY. Don't let my mammy hear you talking like that.

HELEN. Talking like what?

CATHIE. Nothing.

HELEN (*to us*). I'm keeping my distance the day. They're worried enough wi'out me showin' them my worry lines. And it's like they know 'cause they keep their distance fae me an all.

MAGGIE (*to us*). We know 'Elen's carrying the weight of it all.

HELEN (*to us*). They riots in Brixton gi' me shivers, watching the polis in their heavy gear stamping on these young fellas, pulling and shoving them. You'll always lose in a situation like that. If the polis hurt you, you've to live wi' the consequences but if you hurt them – you'll end up in the dock, labelled a criminal.

MAGGIE (*to us*). I still don't know why it's supposed to be good to watch the news when it can scare the stuffing out a you.

CB RADIO. Hello, Larkfield.

FINLAY. Aye, Larkfield here. Have you seen something? Are the heavies on their way?

CB RADIO. Oh aye. They're on their way.

MAGGIE. Did he just say what I think he said?

FINLAY. How far away are they? What can you see?

CB RADIO (*distorted*)....double... and... coal truck.

FINLAY. Can you repeat that? I'm no hearing you.

CATHIE. I'm no good wi' violence. If I'd been in France when
    the Nazis invaded, I'd have been one a they collaborators.
    Just shacked up wi' one a them. I'm no brave.

MAGGIE. What do we do, 'Elen?

FINLAY (*to the radio*). I'm still no hearing you.

CATHIE. I'm gonnae go all limp so I'm hard to carry. I seen it
    on the telly.

MAGGIE. I'm gonnae thump anybody who tries to carry me.

CATHIE. In that case, I'm standing behind you.

MAGGIE. How many a them is it, Finlay?

FINLAY. Shh – I'm trying to listen.

MAGGIE. What's the plan, 'Elen? Are you wanting us to form
    a chain?

HELEN. I dunno, I... I'm no wanting anybody to get hurt.

MAGGIE. So what do we do?

HELEN. –

    HELEN *is paralysed. The other three clump together looking
    outside.*

MAGGIE. I can see them.

CATHIE. Where?

MAGGIE. There. See.

CATHIE. That's a double-decker bus. How's that them?

HELEN. That's a whole row of double-decker buses.

MAGGIE. And a coal truck.

CATHIE. Why would the Americans send their heavies round in a coal truck?

HELEN. It's no the Americans. It's the miners.

CATHIE. Aye, that makes more sense.

HELEN. Is that Patrick? Getting off that first bus?

That's my man's cousin, Pat. Fae Lithgows.

MAGGIE. It's the men fae the yards.

FINLAY puts down the radio, having finally heard the message.

FINLAY. Shipyard men and miners. Folk on our side.

CATHIE. So the heavies that are on their way are our heavies?

FINLAY. Aye, I think that's what Bridie's son is saying through the static.

MAGGIE. The cavalry are coming!

CATHIE. So are the VF heavies on their way an' all or no?

FINLAY. I'm no sure but if they are, we've got backup.

HELEN. We're no on our own.

MAGGIE. Nae need to feel lonely.

HELEN. Lonely? Who was feeling lonely?

MAGGIE. *Stand and deliver!*

In the original production, 'Stand and Deliver' by Adam and the Ants was sung here, along with the battle bugle from the opening.

HELEN. Patrick Clark! Is that you?

PAT. Who needs a motor when you can get around wi' your own double-decker bus?!

HELEN. How?

PAT. Western SNP Garage up at Ladyburn gied us buses free a charge. All arranged by the Transport and General Workers' Union.

HELEN. It's better than a caravan, that's for sure!

I cannae find the words to thank them.

PAT. Well you better find them quick 'cause they're wanting a speech.

HELEN. I'll no stand for any wolf-whistling. Support or no. A single whistle, I'll walk away.

PAT. There's no gonnae be any a that.

HELEN. There'd better no be. I'm telling you.

PAT. Something's changed when they talk about you these past months. It's no 'they Lee Jeans lassies' no more, they call you workers now.

HELEN. We always were workers.

PAT. You've proved it to them.

HELEN. 'Bout time.

PAT. You've done it your own way and achieved more than the men have in years.

HELEN. I don't know about that. We've no kept our jobs yet.

PAT. You've no lost them either.

HELEN. No yet.

PAT. Now where are these VF heavies? 'Cause we're all spoiling for a fight.

HELEN (*to us*). The Americans didnae show.

MAGGIE (*to us*). Only our pals.

HELEN (*to us*). Friends, camera crews and the provost who finally showed up after months a me making the argument about the machinery belonging to Greenock.

MAGGIE (*to us*). 'Elen got snapped by the paparazzi, her finger in his face, tearing into him. It was class.

HELEN (*to us*). By then I didnae need the provost or naebody. I'd made the argument. Embarrassed the Americans enough that they just wanted out. Word was they were willing to sell and if a buyer could be found, we would keep our jobs. *If.*

Playing the Underdog

*The ensemble unravel their knitted scarf of chains. It is
ridiculously long now. It reads: 'FIVE MONTHS IN'.*

HELEN. Months pass and our only offer is from a barraboy
who thinks he's gonnae get his jeans made for nothing.
Nerves start up then. How long will the public stay on our
side?

MR SMITH. Five months is a long time to play the underdog.

HELEN. What are you saying, Mr Smith?

MR SMITH. I'm suggesting that the tide has turned. And
I don't think you're gonnae win this.

HELEN. We.

MR SMITH. Sorry?

HELEN. You're our union. If we lose, you lose. You don't think
'we're' gonnae win this. Unless we're no a 'we' any more.
Unless you're dropping us. Is that why you've got me here
today?

MR SMITH. I'm not willing to tarnish the reputation of this
union with the militant groups you are associating with.

HELEN. How am I associating wi' militant groups?

MR SMITH. War On Want, Big Flame, Right to Work – they've
all been at the factory, pulling your strings from the start.
I've heard you speak. Every word is out of the Right to Work
playbook and they are violent militants.

HELEN. You're wrong, Mr Smith. I'm no puppet. I wisnae telt
what to say. I was just born in a house wi' twelve to a family.
And back then we didnae have National Health. Before
you've paid off the bill for one wean, the next one is ill and
you've no option but to borrow the money fae somewhere to
pay for it.

I came here the day on a train paid for wi' soap-powder
vouchers but the year before I was born, my father joined

the hunger march wi' other unemployed men a Scotland and marched all the way down here on foot. And he didnae keep well, my father. Emphysema. Years he'd spent breathing the fumes fae the welding a pipes at Hughes in Port Glasgow before he was laid off. But he marched. Nothing would stop him marching. He died before Maggie Thatcher bagged the top job but he had her card. 'I wilnae be here to see the harm she causes.'

I'm no puppet, Mr Smith, I'm just my daddy's daughter. Wanting the same as they wanted back then. A job. One for mysel and ones for those around me. There's a hundred and forty of us left and I'm telling you, we'll win this wi' or without you. 'Cause I've got lassies going out and raising funds, drumming up support. If you saw these lassies, Mr Smith, you wouldnae think a dropping us. You'd know they lassies are gonnae win us this thing.

Winning Us This Thing

A nervous MAGGIE *walks towards the audience, who as far as* MAGGIE *is concerned are an intimidating collection of SNP members.*

MAGGIE (*as Gladys from* Hi-de-Hi!). Hello, campers!… I'm doing her off *Hi-de-Hi!* Gladys. Don't know why – it's the one thing my sister telt me, she said 'You cannae do your Welsh accent at an SNP conference.' Apparently bad things happen when I do it. Richard Burton divorces Elizabeth Taylor again. And Shirley Bassey loses her diamonds-are-forever. And Tom Jones forgets to leave his hat on. Focus, Maggie.

…We're fighting for a job I didnae even want when I got it. It's a scary job when you first start, a wee lassie straight out a school faced wi' these big industrial machines. And I done the waistbands. It gets fed through a folder and you bring up the denim to meet it and then you press the pedal.

And it joins the two thegither and you cut the material left over wi' a guillotine at the back. It's a big blade and it comes down hard. So if your fingers are under that – and sometimes they can be if the pressure is off or the guard is slack – if your fingers are under when that blade comes down, your granny'll be knitting you fingerless winter gloves.

If we don't win this thing, if we lose our jobs, I think I'll know then what it feels like to have your fingers under that blade. 'Cause they American managers trying to take all our jobs, they're the blade. And we're no waste material. They shouldnae be allowed to cut us away just 'cause they want more green in their wallets. Working people are no offcuts fit only for the bin.

So I'm here in Aberdeen to ask you for any money you can spare.

And change…

I'm here in Edinburgh to ask your workers' cooperative for any support you can gi' us.

And change…

I'm here in Stirling to rally support.

And change…

I'm here in Burnley asking for your help.

And change…

I'm here… Where am I?

CATHIE. You're home, you bam. Just in time for the big day.

MAGGIE. I feel dizzy wi' all the travelling.

CATHIE. Don't play the victim. You and Cath'rine are having the time a your life while I'm stuck here drawing up rotas for a hundred and forty workers.

MAGGIE. You wouldnae want to trade places. Couldnae see you staying at the big house we stayed last week where they were all running about in their knickers, smoking that much wacky baccy, Cath'rine and I felt giddy wi' it.

CATHIE. That the one wi' the dormitory wi' the beds all in a line like a morgue, aye?

MAGGIE. I had to sleep wi' my towel round my head like a turban 'cause I didnae trust the pillowcase.

CATHIE. Better than the wee house you stayed in without a lock on the toilet so you had to pee wi' your foot against the door. And all they weans trying to get in there wi' you.

MAGGIE. They weans stole my pyjamas!

CATHIE. Out a the vanity case our mammy packed for you – aye. You know, Maggie, it cannae all be hanging out wi' celebrities telling you to / up the gun!

MAGGIE. / Up the gun! That Vanessa Redgrave's something else. I mind watching her couple year ago getting booed in her Oscar speech for speaking out for Palestine and I thought she must feel bad but then I met her and realised she's frightened a nothing.

You really do know all the stories. How?

CATHIE. 'Cause I may be good at staying here and doing cooking rotas but when you and Cath'rine come back wi' all your banter, it's, well, it's –

MAGGIE. The highlight a your day?!

MAGGIE's said it ironically but it's clear from CATHIE's response that she's hit the nail on the head.

MAGGIE. Are you proud a me, Cathie Wallace?

CATHIE. Are you proud a yoursel?

MAGGIE. Aye. It's like Cath'rine said. I feel like one a my daddy's doos.

CATHIE. Look like one and all. Could have at least have put a brush through your hair for the big day.

MAGGIE. What you going on about – big day? Is there a rally I've forgotten about?

CATHIE. Do you never read the rota? I wrote it in big letters.

The ensemble hold up a knitted banner with wedding bells and crowns: 'SIX MONTHS IN: THE ROYAL WEDDING'.

The ensemble put on tiny Union Jack bowler hats.

MAGGIE. Oh my God, she looks like something out a *Cinderella*. Look at the size a that train.

FINLAY. She looks like wan a they dolls you put over a toilet roll.

CATHIE. I think she looks like an angel.

FINLAY. You've to wonder why an angel like her would marry a man wi' ears that big you could hang a duffel coat on them.

CATHIE. Aye but he'll be King one day, ears or no.

HELEN. Have you no got college work to do, Finlay?

FINLAY. I'm just sitting down for five minutes!

CATHIE. Look at the size a that church. Are you no wanting to watch this, 'Elen?

HELEN. Why should I? I've never met either a them and I'm no likely to.

CATHIE. Aye but do you no want to see how pretty it is?

HELEN. It'd better be pretty. They're saying it's costing fifty-seven million pound. That's our money, mind. I've better things to spend my time on than expensive fairytales.

MAGGIE. Isn't fairytales exactly what you're spending your time on, 'Elen? Have you had any more offers on the table wi' storybook sums?

HELEN. Last offer was fae a total chancer right enough. There's nothing made-up about the offer we've got on the table the noo.

MAGGIE has no interest in the wedding now…

MAGGIE. So you think this is mebbe the one that'll stick?

HELEN (*for* MAGGIE *only*). A secret buyer giving guarantees that all hundred and forty workers left in this fight will have jobs if the sale goes through. I don't want to say anything until I know for sure but… it's looking promising.

MAGGIE. So what happens if they buy the place?

HELEN. We'd have our jobs back. Get back to our normal lives.

MAGGIE. No more meetings or marches or interviews?

HELEN. Naw. All that would be done wi'. We'd get on wi' doing the sewing like we used to. I'm no getting my hopes up till I've seen it signed and sealed but it's looking good. Keep it under your hat.

Beat.

MAGGIE. I'm no wanting it to end, 'Elen.

HELEN. How do you mean?

MAGGIE. I'm no wanting all this to stop.

HELEN. Aye you do.

MAGGIE. Naw, 'Elen. And I cannae believe you do either. After everything you've done, speaking to famous folk – boring famous mebbe but famous all the same. Getting invited to Sweden and America and who knows where else. Having your photo never out the paper. You're no telling me you want a gi' all that up?

HELEN. I do, Maggie. See if I'd known at the beginning we'd still be doing this all these months on – I'd never have started.

MAGGIE. These past months have been the best a my life. You wanted me to prove mysel and I did. How can I go back to being who I was before that? It's no fair.

HELEN. Fair?! There's six a they hunger strike boys dead now and two more who've already starved themselves longer than the first. They'll be dead in days. That'll be eight a them. And where's the prime minister in all this? She's sitting in her navy pillbox hat in St Paul's wi' all the other rich folk, delighted that the rest a us are so distracted watching a big fancy wedding and waving our flags, that we're no taking to the streets shouting about how unfair this country really is. It'll never change, no now, no in forty year fae now. All this, sitting in, fighting for our jobs. We were never gonnae win. We were just trying no to lose, Maggie!

I don't know who this secret buyer is but if it's a good enough deal, if it gets us out a this mess, if it means we don't lose, I'll take it wi' both hands and say all the thank-yous they need to hear.

Bob Charters' Surprise

BOB CHARTERS. You're welcome.

HELEN. You? Wee Bob Charters has bought out the Americans?

The ensemble wear ridiculous knitted onesies, which read: 'SEVEN MONTHS IN'.

BOB CHARTERS. Don't look so surprised. I've managed this factory, I know it inside and out. Me and a couple of other managers did the sums and made an offer.

HELEN. So it is profitable, our factory is profitable?

BOB CHARTERS. Course it's profitable.

HELEN. And you couldnae have told me that seven month ago?

BOB CHARTERS. Let's not look backwards, Helen. You've won. You've saved your jobs. Enjoy your moment – you're a hero.

Working-Class Hero

In the original production, the company sang John Lennon's 'Working Class Hero'. It's a melancholic melody at the best of times but even more so in this moment with Lennon's death still so raw. HELEN *is processing the battle of the last seven months.*

FINLAY, *wearing a Palestinian keffiyeh, joins* HELEN.

FINLAY. What are you doing in here all by yersel?

HELEN. Just taking a moment.

FINLAY. Has something bad happened?

HELEN. No.

I was just thinking, it was nice a them to let me look like this. Like I was.

FINLAY. What do you mean? How else would you look?

HELEN. Old.

I'm eighty-nine, son. All this was forty-five year ago.

Something shifts. We are now outside of time and place.

FINLAY. Don't be daft.

HELEN. It's 2026, son. They've asked me to look back at our story. About how we won.

FINLAY. We won?

HELEN. Aye. Sort of.

FINLAY. You don't seem very happy about it?

HELEN. It was a long time ago for me. I've seen where we all end up.

FINLAY. 2026?! I don't remember 2026…

HELEN. That's 'cause you don't live to see it, my love. You died in 2020. A year older than your daddy was when the cancer got him.

But what you achieved in the time you had… You went on to manage factories bigger than this. In Sri Lanka, Bangkok and Boston. And you'd fly me out and have me in these expensive hotels and if I made noise about it, you'd say that was what it was all for. To spoil me.

FINLAY. I managed factories?

HELEN. Aye, and you were fair, mind. You did right by them you employed.

FINLAY. I turned out alright then? That's a turn-up for the books.

HELEN. No really. I always knew you could do it. Look at what you achieved while all this was going on.

FINLAY. That's what I came to tell you. But I guess you already know.

HELEN. Let's play it out. It's a happy memory.

FINLAY *agrees and replays the first two lines of the scene before* HELEN *broke out of it.*

FINLAY. What are you doing in here all by yersel?

HELEN. Just taking a moment.

FINLAY. I've been looking for you. I've news.

HELEN. That makes two a us. (*Pointing to his scarf.*) What are you wearing?

FINLAY. George Galloway gied me it. He's big on Palestinian liberation.

HELEN. Less politics and more college work, please.

FINLAY. That's my news.

HELEN. You passed your course?

FINLAY. More than that. I was made Top Boy.

HELEN. Top Boy?!

FINLAY. Tell me your news is good an' all.

HELEN. They Americans have accepted an offer. Fae Bob Charters of all folk. He's taking this factory on himsel', wi' two other colleagues. He's got a big order that will last us three years at least. A hundred and forty jobs guaranteed for that time. A job for every worker who's stayed the course a the strike. I've the list a names here.

The names of the 140 people who fought and kept their jobs are projected (or at least all of the names we could gather from a media callout and the understandably fallible memories of the workers we were able to consult).

This story belongs to them.

Hessie Adams, Ella Agnew, John Aitken, Alec Anderson, Carol Anderson, Ina Anderson, Joyce Anderson, Kay Anderson, Christina Arkley, Patricia Arkley, Linda Bell, Bridie Bellingham, Marie Bolton, Martina Bradley, Margaret Brown, Mary Bryce, Catherine Burden, Betty Burns, Elizabeth Burns, Liz Canning, Tricia Cannon, Senga Carroll, Helen Church, Joan Clocherty, Wendy Couper, Sadie Cowan, Jean Cracknell, Agnes Danison, Betty Daytons, Christine Dempster, Margaret Derrick, Anne Docherty, Anne Dominick, Alice Donaghy, Brenda Donnelly, Anne Duffy, John Duffy, Carol Galbraith, Linda Galbraith, Mary Galbraith, Betty Gatens, Jenny Gillespie, Margaret Gillan, Lynne Grierson, Bridie Groenewald, Jacqueline Groenewald, Ellen Harrington, Linda Herald, Theresa Houston, Lynne Ingleby, Catherine Jenkins, Maria Jenkins, Marie Jenkins, Alison Kavanagh, Elaine Kavanagh, Margaret Kilbride, Linda Kinsella, Mary Lepick, Liz Logan, George Malcolm, Hugh Malcolm, May Martin, Heather McBride, Linda McCabe, Maria McCabe, Sheena McCabe, Christine McCafferty, Ina McCahill, Kay McCahill, Joan McClurg, Carol McDade, Ruth McDevitt, Colleen McDowell, Eleanor McGowan, Isabel McGowan, Sandra McGowan, Celia McGrath, Marie McGrath, Ruby McIntosh, Christine McKernan, Linda McLachlan, Mary McLaughlin, Tricia McLaughlin, Sandra McLean, Thomas McLean, Agnes McMillan, Ann McPhee, Shirley McPhee, Norman McNeill, Linda McRobie, Margaret McRobie, Alan McWilliams, Catherine Miller, Maureen Miller, May Miller, Frank Mitchell, Mary Mitchell, Wilma Mitchell, Marie Mooney, Trisha Molloy, Finlay Monaghan, Helen Monaghan, Linda Monaghan, Marie Monaghan, Anne O'Neil, Elaine Patterson, Elizabeth Patterson, Isabel Petterson, Harry Queen, Hilda Queens, Tricia Queens, Catherine Robertson, Elizabeth Robertson, Christine Ruffel, Elizabeth Sassarini, Unity Sinclair, Kathleen Kinsella Spires,

Wilma Swan, Anne Swandell, Betty Swandell, Catherine Swandell, Margaret Swandell, Carol Sweenie, Grace Todd, Linda Todd, Rosemary Thompson, Cathie Wallace, Maggie Wallace, Agnes Wallis, Annemarie White, Carol Willans, Linda Willans, Isobel Williams.

FINLAY. Mam, that's amazing. How long before our former union comes knocking?

HELEN. They can knock themselves into a coma. We're going wi' the guys that put on the buses when we needed some solidarity. We're going wi' the Transport and General Workers' Union.

FINLAY. Go on yersel, Mammy!

HELEN. Top Boy. All this time doing your studies while on the night shift here. You're some boy. You should be running this place.

FINLAY. Mebbe I will one day.

HELEN. There's no stopping you. I'm that proud a you, son.

FINLAY. Proud a me? Look at you. What did that newspaper call you – Joan a Arc in blue denim jeans or was it 'Elen a Troy?

HELEN. 'Elen a Port Glasgow more like.

FINLAY. You did it, Mammy. We won. You're a working-class hero.

CATHIE *and* MAGGIE *join* HELEN *and* FINLAY.

CATHIE. No Lennon please. It's too sad. This should be a happy moment, shouldn't it?

MAGGIE. That depends on what we're up to in 2026.

HELEN. You two are doing good. I think you could even say you like each other. You were tight when your kids were wee.

CATHIE. Bet you still annoy me but.

MAGGIE. You annoy me more.

FINLAY. I don't think we should be ending on Lennon. What about 'Celebration' by Kool and the Gang – that came out in '81?

HELEN. Thing is the jobs didnae last. Thatcher's free market killed it in three years. I saw the writing on the wall and went into home help the year before it all shut up.

MAGGIE. I bet I was top a the list when they made their redundancies.

HELEN. Naebody would gi' you a job 'cause all the speaking you did marked you out as a militant. You had to go to Jersey where naebody knew you to get work. Being part a this wisnae something to shout about back then. I lied when I was recognised by the wee old ladies I was looking after. Didnae want to scare them.

You work wi' folk wi' dementia now, Maggie. Lot a the workers went into caring jobs. We were the ones picking up the pieces in the pandemic while Boris was partying.

MAGGIE. Who the hell is Boris?

HELEN. He's old news. New lot in now. Labour but you wouldnae know it. Business still comes first.

CATHIE. So why are we telling the story at all – if nothing changed?

HELEN. Stuff did change for a bit. There were two other sit-ins in Scottish factories after us, Lovable in Cumbernauld and Plessey in Bathgate. They were places where the workers were mostly women. Their bosses were being unfair, closing them for no reason, moving abroad, and throwing them on the dole. I advised them and they won and all. So no just our jobs were saved, but another six-hundred-odd on top a that.

CATHIE. You were like a sequin on a bit a black cord. Giving folk hope.

FINLAY. Should have gone into politics, Mammy. Like Jimmy Reid and Jimmy Airlie. Then things would a changed.

HELEN. Aye, mebbe. That wisnae what I knew. It was the 1980s and the only woman I knew in politics was one I hated.

FINLAY. Don't let's end the story there. On a downer.

MAGGIE. He's right. We need to show them the good bits. We won.

HELEN. Telling you all the news, the morning after I heard. That was the best bit.

CATHIE. And the party after at Greenock Town Hall.

HELEN. Oh aye.

FINLAY. Where we finally got to drink they crates a booze we were gied back at the start.

HELEN. Aye and the men who I tasked to carry them – including cousin Pat – were half-cut by the time they got them to the hall.

VIPs

Greenock Town Hall. The ensemble are head-to-toe in denim, which reads: 'AUGUST 1981 – WE WON!'

HELEN. The polis sergeant came to find me. I thought, oh hell, what's Maggie done now? But he came to shake my hand.

POLICE SERGEANT. They wanted you to break the law. Anything, even the most minor offence, we were under strict instructions to act and we were watching you day and night. If you'd done a single thing wrong, we'd have seen it and we'd have come down hard.

HELEN. Aye, that's what I thought. I knew I had to keep folk in line.

POLICE SERGEANT. That was a lot of folk to keep in line. You're some woman. I think the provost is wanting a word.

HELEN. That man. Nae trace a him when I need him but he always shows up when it's party time. Hope there's no cameras to snap me laying into him this time.

She goes to leave but stops.

Thank you. I needed to hear that.

FINLAY. Alright, Maggie.

MAGGIE. Finbar! How's tricks?

FINLAY. I had a dream about you. We were getting married and you were wearing this big frock.

MAGGIE. Diana big?

FINLAY. Close. And I was terrified but then I looked down and you were wearing Doc Martens and I wisnae scared any more. I woke up and I thought – I'm gonnae ask out Maggie Wallace.

Beat. It's a no from MAGGIE *and* FINLAY *knows it.*

Then I remembered that you're more J.R. than Bobby when it comes to Ewings.

MAGGIE. Think you're a Bobby, do you?

FINLAY. Bobby Ewing wishes he looked like me. You heard fae Jimmy?

MAGGIE. Naw. We're finally drinking the booze he kept going on about.

FINLAY. Saw him out the other night. He gied me the thumbs-up fae across the street. Will you ask him out, now this is over?

MAGGIE. My mammy'd kill me! Anyway, things I liked about Jimmy was he made me feel important.

FINLAY. And you don't need him to feel like that now?

MAGGIE. You're kidding? Everybody is here the night, celebrating us. Important? We're bloody VIPs! I heard some a they lassies bragging that they were classmates wi' you at Bayview. You should go and dance wi' one a them – make their night.

HELEN. Aye you should.

You should, Finlay.

FINLAY. How? Do I end up marrying one a them?

Yep.

HELEN. I'm saying nothing.

FINLAY. Thought you said I'm headed for Sri Lanka, Bangkok and Boston?

HELEN. Aye but you're headed there wi' a Greenock lassie.

FINLAY. Which one?

MAGGIE. Ask a few to dance and see which one you like best.

FINLAY. Aye alright then.

Is it Cathie?

CATHIE. Is it hell. I'll dance wi' you but.

They dance.

MAGGIE. I'm sorry, 'Elen.

HELEN. What for?

MAGGIE. Doing your nut in.

HELEN. Oh aye, plenty a times you've been a thorn in my side.

But you've done me proud.

MAGGIE. Have I?

HELEN. Course you have.

The others have faded out so it's just MAGGIE *and* HELEN.

MAGGIE. I feel like I could do anything. Change things. Imagine if folk like us could change things, 'Elen. Imagine what the world would be like.

MAGGIE *fades out too, leaving* HELEN *alone on stage.*

HELEN. Aye, that's a good thought. I'm gonnae imagine that.

A Nick Hern Book

Stand & Deliver: The Lee Jeans Sit-In first published in Great Britain as a paperback original in 2026 by Nick Hern Books Limited, The Glasshouse, 49a Goldhawk Road, London W12 8QP, in association with National Theatre of Scotland and Tron Theatre Company

Stand & Deliver: The Lee Jeans Sit-In copyright © 2026 Frances Poet

Frances Poet has asserted her moral right to be identified as the author of this work

Cover image courtesy of Trinity Mirror

Designed and typeset by Nick Hern Books, London
Printed in Great Britain by Mimeo Ltd, Huntingdon, Cambridgeshire PE29 6XX

A CIP catalogue record for this book is available from the British Library

ISBN 978 1 83904 585 1

www.nickhernbooks.co.uk/environmental-policy

Nick Hern Books' authorised representative in the EU is
Easy Access System Europe – Mustamäe tee 50, 10621 Tallinn, Estonia
email gpsr.requests@easproject.com

www.nickhernbooks.co.uk

@nickhernbooks